R0061531273

01/2012

D1073553

THE DESERT FATHERS

Peter H. Görg

The Desert Fathers

Anthony and the Beginnings of Monasticism

Translated by
Michael J. Miller

IGNATIUS PRESS   SAN FRANCISCO

Original German edition:
Die Wüsten Väter: Antonius und die Anfänge des Mönchtums
© 2008 by Sankt Ulrich Verlag GmbH, Augsburg, Germany

All the quotations from *The Life of Anthony* are taken from
The Life of Antony: The Coptic Life *and* The Greek Life
© 2003 by Cistercian Publications, Kalamazoo, MI
Published by Liturgical Press, Collegeville, MN
Used with permission

Cover photo:
St. Catherine Monastery near Mt. Sinai, Egypt
© Luke1138/iStockphoto

Cover design by Roxanne Mei Lum

ISBN: 978-1-58617-445-3
Library of Congress Control Number 2010937198
Printed in the United States of America ∞

To my priest-friend
Wilbert Dornoff

CONTENTS

INTRODUCTION

"They build houses as though they were going to live forever, and they eat as though they were going to die tomorrow!" This description of his fellow citizens goes back to
one of the Greek philosophers of antiquity, but it could
just as well have originated in our day. At the same time it
expresses something of the general human endeavor to settle down in this world and not to miss anything. What mat-
ters, supposedly, is not the number of years but rather the
intensity of one's life, by which is generally meant in turn
the greatest possible potential for experiencing pleasure. Since
this attitude can be found in all ages and in all places, the
very existence of the Christian monk represents a protest.
This protest is directed against a hedonistic society that sees
its sole purpose for existence in maximizing pleasure and in
fun, and likewise against a form of narrow-minded bour-
geois existence that is satisfied with managing a pleasant
life in this world. From this perspective the monk is coun-
tercultural, someone who is striving precisely for another
sort of life.

The very term "monk" can be interpreted in several ways,
which at the same time reflect the living reality. Whereas
the translation "alone" (in Greek *mónos*) reminds us more
of the hermit, we can also speak—as John Cassian, for example, does—about someone who leads a "singular" or
"uncommon life". The Christian monk knows only one
goal: the absolute submission of his whole being to God by
imitating Christ. This imitation assumes its concrete form
chiefly in following the so-called evangelical counsels of

obedience, poverty, and celibacy [*Ehelosigkeit*]. So as to be able to live out this imitation of Christ radically and totally, the monk leaves the "world". He renounces all natural ties and at the same time frees himself from those temptations that accompany material possession.

The origin of Christian monasticism can be seen in the Gospel itself, in Christ's invitations to leave everything for his name's sake (cf. Mt 19:29), and likewise in the example of the Redeemer, of the God-man who in his earthly life modeled the aforementioned counsels. And already in the Acts of the Apostles we encounter monastic elements, when it is reported about the early Christian community that they were united in personal poverty, in fellowship, and in the praise of God (cf. Acts 2:42–47; 4:32). Here we find also the beginnings of a special virginal state of life (Acts 21:9) and the first indications of asceticism. The ascetical way of life was realized in the first two Christian centuries chiefly in two forms. First there was itinerant asceticism, which was based primarily on the Scripture passages about the sending forth of the first disciples (see Lk 10:1–12) who roamed the world on missionary journeys. These ascetics are said to have been influential well into the early medieval period, although they were not always regarded favorably by the Church because of their sometimes disorderly way of life. The other and most common form was exemplified by those ascetics who lived in the family and the Christian community and formed, so to speak, their inner circle and spiritual center. They led an unmarried life, ready to give to the poor and to the community everything beyond what they needed to support themselves. Abstinence from wine and meat can be found in this early phase also, and among the ascetical women, who probably originated with the enrolled widows, one can discern a special vow of continence. As time went on, this asceticism, which consisted in renouncing food, sleep, and other amenities of life, naturally required reflection and correction again and again to keep it from falling short of its actual goal of perfection and becoming an exercise in hostility to the body.

It was not until the third century that a movement began in which the ascetics increasingly detached themselves from their social surroundings and separated themselves spatially from the world so as to lead the life of a hermit. This was the origin of eremitical monasticism, which was already accompanied by a certain monastic garb that was distinguished by its simplicity. The designation "hermit" comes from the Greek. Whereas the corresponding adjective *erēmos* means "solitary" or "living in seclusion", the noun is used for both "solitude" and "desert", which brings us directly to our topic. In Latin the loan-word *eremita* acquired the meaning "recluse", which is familiar to us. Early on these hermits also recognized the need for a spiritual father so as not to go astray in their asceticism and spiritual life. He acquired the Greek title "Abbas", which in the time of Jesus was used to address the father of a family. Among the Desert Fathers one figure was especially preeminent: Abbas Anthony, who is also known as Anthony the Hermit [and Anthony the Abbot and Anthony the Great].

In the year 2006 the Church observed the 1650th anniversary of the death of the saintly hermit and abbot Anthony. Because of his greatness and importance he exemplifies the beginning of monastic life. This book is meant to contribute in some small way toward making Anthony the Great better known again to twenty-first-century Christians as well. Hence the focus of this presentation is the life and work of the saint. Incidentally from time to time there will be explanatory remarks to make it easier for the reader to understand the unfamiliar world of the ascetic. Moreover, in presenting the life of Anthony it will be necessary to call to mind again truths of the faith that have almost been buried in the sands of time, for instance, with regard to the possibility of miracles or the existence of purely spiritual beings. In order to corroborate the credibility of miraculous events we will refer in the appropriate places to similar incidents in the lives of modern saints. This presentation thereby clearly sets itself apart from many publications in recent decades that either completely deny the possibility and factuality of God's miraculous intervention in our world (in other words, the irruption of transcendence into immanence), or interpret it in purely symbolic terms, or else relegate it to the realm of psychology.

Scarcely any other saint has fascinated and inspired the artists of all ages as much as the Egyptian hermit. Painters such as Hieronymus Bosch, Matthias Grünewald, Pieter Brueghel, Lukas Cranach, or even Salvador Dalí and Max Ernst repeatedly dealt with motifs from the life of the Abbot, and in literature there are numerous references and allusions to this great man, who was the bedrock of asceticism. Being an important saint of the Church he can help the faithful—despite or precisely because of the strangeness of his foreign extraction, his way of life, and his thought—as a model along the path to sanctity. His experiences in the spiritual life and the ideas derived from it have a timeless beauty and validity.

For many centuries, furthermore, Christians in the East and the West have confidently turned to this saint and have experienced the help of his intercession. This book is meant to encourage all its readers to do so also, especially those, of course, who honor the hermit as their patron saint (Anthony, Antoinette, Anton, Toni, and so forth) or the patron of their parish.

The second part of this book presents other great figures who either were themselves among the Desert Fathers or were inspired by them. We will hear about the primordial hermit, Paul of Thebes, who is said to have sought seclusion in the desert many years even before Anthony. We will learn how real monasteries developed under the direction of Pachomius and how the monks discovered life in community as cenobites. The story of Syrian monasticism and of its particular exponents, like the pillar dweller Simeon, will be related, as well as the history of the monks in Asia Minor, headed by the great theologian and bishop Basil.

Although we then turn also to the further development of monasticism and thus leave the desert behind, it always remains in the background, because the entire monastic movement relied again and again on its sources in the desert. Indeed, the great promoters of monasticism and asceticism in the West often had one thing in common: in their early years they visited the monks in Egypt and Palestine. They set out on the arduous journey to visit the Desert Fathers and their disciples. And we too want to set out now on that journey.

EGYPT

Egypt—the mere name of this country is still indescribably fascinating even today. It immediately gives rise to mental images of a culture that is thousands of years old, which we associate with the building of the pyramids, the early hieroglyphic form of writing, and a well-defined belief in a life hereafter. And who could forget the mighty Nile, the main artery of transportation and the center of Egyptian life to this day? This country, which is bounded on the east by the Red Sea and on the west by Libya, serves as the bridge between Asia and Africa; however it is also inseparably connected with the history of Israel and early Christianity. The name "Egypt" is mentioned 750 times in Sacred Scripture. At the same time the relationship between Egypt and Israel was always ambivalent. On the one hand it was the land of slavery from which Moses led the chosen people. Yet on the other hand Egypt also served as a place of refuge. Thus the earliest of the patriarchs, Abraham, found there a friendly reception and food during a time of great famine (see Gen 12:10), and centuries later the Holy Family would find shelter in that same place while they were fleeing from Herod.

After the fall of the Pharaohs, Egypt came under the rule of various empires. Alexander the Great annexed it to his empire in 332 B.C., and for almost three centuries after his death the country along the Nile was ruled by the Ptolemies, who were likewise Greek. During this period the Mediterranean port city of Alexandria developed into the center of literature and learning in antiquity. The legendary library of Alexandria was privileged to call for its own the largest collection of books at that time. From 30 B.C. to A.D. 641 or 642 Egypt was a province of the mighty Roman Empire and supplied it with grain, spices, jewels, and precious metals.

While the Romans were concerned about extending their empire and increasing their prosperity and prestige in the world, the Eternal Word, unnoticed by them, took flesh in the little province of Judea. Whereas in Egypt gods were still being worshipped in the form of animals, the one true God humbled himself in Bethlehem and took on human form. Moreover, the Creator himself became true man, like us in all things except sin. Later legends recount that during the flight of the Holy Family to Egypt pagan idols were toppled as the God-man was carried past them. Yet Egypt would fall back again into the darkness of paganism for a short time. Only after the Resurrection of the Redeemer and the descent of the third Divine Person, the Holy Spirit, did the apostles rush out into the pagan world, spreading the light of the Gospel. Tradition has it that the Evangelist Mark, a disciple of the Head of the apostles, brought the Good News of salvation as far as Alexandria, and that city became one of the leading patriarchal churches. To this day the Coptic "Pope" regards himself as the successor of that Evangelist. From Alexandria the Christian teaching spread throughout Egypt and the pagan gods were unmasked as demons.

ANTHONY OF EGYPT—
ABBOT AND STAR OF THE DESERT

In the midst of this process of Christianization of pagan Egypt, Saint Anthony was born; his life and work will be the focus of our considerations. Besides the titles already mentioned, Anthony received also the honorific title "the Great"; anyone who wants to study him in greater depth must first inquire about the sources that tell about him. It was the great bishop and confessor Athanasius of Alexandria who recorded the life of this saint shortly after 356 at the request of several monks from Gaul or Italy. The original text of the *Vita Antonii* (*Life of Anthony*) was written in the Greek language, but even before the Middle Ages it was translated into Latin (in 373 by Evagrios of Antioch), Syrian, Coptic, Armenian, Georgian, Old Slavonic, and Ethiopian. The influence of the *Vita Antonii* on hagiography (writings about the lives of the saints) was impressive. For the West it was the first encounter with Eastern monasticism, and Anthony himself became the personification of Christian asceticism and the father of monks and hermits. Artists in every age, down to the recent past, have been inspired above all by the saint's battles with demons and have made them appear before the eyes of viewers in phantasmagorical paintings. At this point we must emphasize that the *Life of Anthony* is not the product of pious legends and hearsay. The authorship of the saintly bishop Athanasius can be accepted without a doubt, and he was able to rely on his own meetings and conversations with Anthony. Although Athanasius adopted stylistic elements from other *Life of Anthony*'s, that should be no reason to question the reliability of what he has handed down. Therefore the *Vita Antonii* will serve as the primary source in our presentation of Anthony's life as well.

We should also give a brief sketch of the biographer's life. Athanasius the Great was born around 295 in Alexandria and earned the honorific title "Father of Orthodoxy", which is to say, [the Father] of Right Doctrine, of Right Belief. In 319 he became a deacon and the secretary of Bishop Alexander of Alexandria, whom he accompanied in 325 to the Council of Nicaea. After Alexander's death in 328 Athanasius was elected his successor and was consecrated a bishop on June 8, 328. Already at the aforementioned Council he had proved to be an extremely brilliant defender of the Christian faith against the erroneous teachings of Arius, who denied the true divinity of Christ and his consubstantiality with God the Father. Broad sectors of the Christian world had been infected by this unchristian doctrine. His opponents even succeeded in having Athanasius banished several times because of his defense of the Nicene doctrine; he had to endure living in exile for a total of seventeen years. He spent his first exile in Trier. The second, during the years 338–346, led him to Rome, Northern Italy, Trier, and Illyria. He spent the next three exiles in the Egyptian and Libyan deserts. During these disputes Athanasius visited Anthony several times and sought his counsel and his help. Not until 366 was the bishop finally able to return to Alexandria, where he stayed until his death on May 2, 373. He did not live to see the Church's definitive victory over Arianism, which is very closely connected with the Council of Constantinople in the year 381. Besides his polemical writings, Athanasius became widely known through his Easter Letters and his *Life of Anthony*.

The *Life of Anthony* by Bishop Athanasius is supplemented by a second source, the so-called *Apophthegmata Patrum* (*Sayings of the Fathers*). This is a collection of sayings of various Desert Fathers that were compiled by their respective disciples. The sayings were handed down in Greek, Coptic, Armenian, and Syrian. In their original form they contain chiefly traditions of the ascetical monks from the middle of the fourth to the middle of the fifth centuries. These sayings, anecdotes, and parables from the lives of the monks are profoundly spiritual and are often cited as an authority, for instance by Benedict of Nursia. In the most familiar collection of Greek texts—Migne's *Patrologia Graeca*—only thirty-eight *apophthegmata* are recorded under the name of Saint Anthony, whereas he is also mentioned in the traditions attributed to other monks. Moreover, several letters from the saint are preserved, which cannot be discussed individually here.

We find further information about the life and work of the saintly hermit Anthony in the *Historia Lausiaca* by the Christian writer Palladius. Originally from Galatia, Palladius, who later became a priest and a bishop, traveled when he was scarcely twenty years old to Egypt in order to learn about the monastic communities there. He spent an especially long time in the Nitrian Desert and became closely associated with the influential monk Evagrius Ponticus. In addition Palladius visited the Christian monks in the Holy Land and was consecrated a bishop in Asia Minor at the beginning of the fifth century. Around the year 420, at the age of fifty-three and in the twentieth year of his episcopate, he composed his collection of monks' lives, which is dedicated to his chamberlain Lausos. Both Egyptian and

Palestinian monks are presented in biographical portraits. In this work Palladius drew in part on his own memories and in part on the verbal communications of others. Perhaps he was able to rely also on the *Historia Monachorum* by Rufinus of Aquileia, who likewise had sought out both the monks of the Nitrian Desert and also those residing in Palestine.

CHILDHOOD AND YOUTH

Anthony was born around the year 251 in central Egypt. Tradition identifies his birthplace as the village of Keman or Koma, which corresponds to modern Queman-el-Arous and is located around one hundred kilometers south of Cairo. In the Roman Empire the persecution of Christians by Emperor Decius was still raging; Decius died in the same year in which Anthony was born. In relating Anthony's childhood, older biographies are fond of embellishments and conjectures that go far beyond the meager information provided by Athanasius. We intend to avoid that here.

Athanasius tells us that Anthony was an Egyptian. In a multinational empire this is not just stating the obvious; special mention of it is made because the child received a Greco-Latin name. Thus Anthony's family belonged to the rural Egyptian population who were referred to as "Copts", which simply means "Egyptians" and later would become a synonym for "Egyptian Christians". To this day their liturgy has preserved the Coptic language that Anthony spoke.

We do not know the names of the child's [Anthony's] parents. But that is not as important as the fact that they were already Christians and raised Anthony as a Christian. Besides that, the parents are described as noble and wealthy. Their properties amounted to more than a hundred hectares [250 acres] of land. Even today that is a very respectable estate, and in the fertile Nile Valley it certainly brought them a very respectable income.

[According to Athanasius,] the child, though, was not particularly concerned about such things and never left his parents' house. If we are to believe this unusual statement by Athanasius, Anthony wanted nothing to do with instruction in reading and writing and also avoided the company of other children. We do not know whether the biographer here was projecting several of the unusual features from the later life of the hermit back into his childhood; we prefer to assume that even as a youth Anthony was inclined to busy himself with higher things than other boys of the same age did. It should also be noted here that his Christian family naturally had to seclude itself during the time of persecution. Anthony continued to have an aversion to worldly wisdom into his advanced old age, which did not prevent him from becoming an adviser to bishops and princes.

Regular church attendance was of course something taken for granted in Christian life even then, and Anthony is depicted as an obedient youth who attentively followed the Scripture readings. Surely the news reached the little Egyptian village that the Roman emperor Valerian had resumed the persecution of the Christians in the year 257 with increased severity. The death penalty was decreed for all clerics who did not sacrifice to the pagan gods or who secretly celebrated the liturgy, and even the Bishop of Alexandria, Dionysius, was incarcerated. Pope Sixtus II suffered martyrdom, as did great numbers of lay people, yet, in contrast to [her response during] the Decian persecution, the Church was now strong and determined, which created for her during the reign of Emperor Gallienus (260–268) and initially even under Diocletian (284–305) a respite that lasted forty years, during which the blood of the martyrs proved to be the fruitful seed of Christianity.

Anthony's parents died at a very early age. Anthony himself was only around eighteen or twenty years old and had only one sister, who was probably significantly younger. Athanasius reports that the young man now took care of his house and his sister. We do not know what plan Anthony had devised for his later life or whether he had any plans at all. It is quite certain, though, that he was already thinking about the ideal of evangelical poverty and considered the [actions of the] apostles, who for Christ's sake left everything, and the faithful of the early Christian community, who laid all their possessions at the feet of the apostles. Not a full six months after the death of his parents, our young Egyptian went to church one day with such thoughts on his mind. As he entered the house of God, he heard the very words that the Lord had spoken to the rich young man: "If you would be perfect, go, sell what you possess and give to the poor, and you will have treasure in heaven; and come, follow me" (Mt 19:21).

CALL TO ASCETICISM

These [foregoing] words [from Matthew's Gospel] moved Anthony with such intensity that he had no doubt whatsoever that they applied to him, the rich young man of Koma. Immediately he left the place of worship and gave away all the land that his family had acquired over several generations to his fellow villagers. He sold all of the movable property and gave the money to the poor according to the Gospel's instruction. He set aside a small part of the money, however, for his younger sister. But that was still not enough! The next time Anthony went to church he heard the Lord's words from the Sermon on the Mount: "Do not be anxious about tomorrow" (Mt 6:34). Now he gave away the remaining sum of money and entrusted his sister to a household of virgins, where she was cared for and raised. Anthony himself, who had detached himself from all earthly possessions, began a life of asceticism that was to form him over the course of several decades.

At this point it is appropriate to present a few thoughts about monasticism. In the wake of the so-called Reformation, a radical critique of the monastic way of life became commonplace and was intensified during the Enlightenment, despite the fact that it had deep foundations in the Gospel. Monks were accused of fleeing the world and disdaining the body, and there were attempts to trace Christian monasticism back to Jewish or pagan models. These theories have proved to be figments of the imagination.

Moreover, the thesis that monasticism arose as a protest against an accommodated state religion, collides with the fact that monasticism had already been in existence for several decades before Christianity gained official recognition and privileges.

Although striving for tranquility, an interior spiritual life, and moral perfection correspond to a basic human desire and hence can be encountered in various cultures and religions, Christian monasticism can be traced to the Gospel as its origin. Its goal is to follow Christ unreservedly, guided by the evangelical counsels of poverty, celibacy, and obedience. Note well that they are counsels and not obligations (it was always the heresies that tried to make a counsel obligatory for everyone). These counsels bestow a freedom that has enabled countless saints in all ages to accomplish outstanding works. The counsels start in precisely those areas where a human being is most intensely afflicted by demonic promptings and temptations—in the desire for possessions, in the satisfaction of carnal appetites, and in egotistical self-assertion—and they raise our sights to that treasure in heaven which neither rust nor moth consumes (Mt 6:19). The contemplative cloister becomes an incalculably effective powerhouse of Christian life and Christian action, which without contemplation would become wearisome activism. It reminds the Church again and again of her primary duties in the world: to work for the glory of God and the salvation of souls. It admonishes all Christians not to become self-satisfied and settled in this world. The renunciation of all those things that we take so much for granted is the most vivid testimony to the Christian hope for a life of true fulfillment—to put it simply, the hope of heaven. From this selfless way of life automatically proceeds care for the poor and the oppressed, and thus it becomes also a source of active love of neighbor. It is probably one of the greatest

follies of the "enlightened" period of history that it tried
to play off contemplation against action, prayer against charity, favoring the second and at the same time depriving it
of its source of power.

But let us return to Anthony. The solitary life was not
invented by our saint, and so at first he sought out other
men who had already practiced asceticism for quite some
time and who let him share in their practical wisdom. Initially he lived in the vicinity of his parents' house and earned
a small income for himself through manual labor. In doing
so he relied on the saying of the Apostle [Paul]: "If any one
will not work, let him not eat" (2 Thess 3:10). Behind this
also was the great wisdom of the monks which is attributed
especially to Saint Benedict and his brief motto "*ora et
labora*"—"pray and work"; moreover it corresponds to the
nature of man as a body-soul composite who needs times
in which the mind and the body are alternately active and
at rest.

According to the *apophthegmata* that have been handed
down, Anthony once stayed in the solitude of the desert
during his later years as well. Suddenly he was overcome by
a strong feeling that his efforts were senseless, and his thoughts
became gloomy. Consequently he begged God, "Lord, I
want to be saved, but my thoughts do not let me alone.
What should I do in my affliction? Where shall I find salvation?" Thereupon he went outside and saw someone like
himself. This unfamiliar figure—Anthony recognized in him
the angel of the Lord—was seated at work. Then he stood
up and prayed, only to sit down again afterward and continue braiding his rope. Then he rose to his feet again to
pray. The angel whom God had sent to instruct Anthony
spoke to the hermit: "Proceed thus and you will be saved."
Anthony was overjoyed by this experience and from then
on lived in that way.

Any money that Anthony did not need for his day-to-day support, he immediately gave to the poor. Another peculiar feature of a monk is his constant prayer, which can take many forms; the Jesus Prayer and the prayer of ardor, or the Prayer of the Heart, have their roots in Eastern monasticism. Furthermore Anthony set about not only hearing the words of Sacred Scripture but also learning them by heart so as to carry them with him always.

In his efforts to make progress along the way of Christian perfection through prayer and asceticism, Anthony assimilated from the numerous role models whom he consulted the best practices in fasting, prayer, generosity, and the love of Christ and soon earned in his village the honorary title "Beloved of God". Yet wherever the pursuit of perfection and of a life in Christ is in earnest, the tempter also makes his presence known, since he regards it as his chief business to detach the human soul from God and to drag it away into eternal damnation. Whereas in recent decades people in many places have bid farewell to the devil, claiming that he is only a mythical figure, the Church has continuously affirmed the existence of Satan and of the other fallen angels, the demons. In this connection, of course, she teaches that even Satan was not originally an evil principle apart from God, but rather was brought into being as something good by the Creator himself but broke with God of his own free will through disobedience and pride. As a result of the Fall and the accompanying loss of sanctifying grace, man was almost defenseless against the devil's temptations until Christ accomplished salvation. Finally Christ appeared to destroy Satan's work and to put the devil in chains. Until Christ's return in glory and the definitive banishment of the Adversary, however, the latter still has a restricted power, with which he tries especially to lead human beings astray from God's ways by his "promptings". Naturally, internal psychological elements play an important role also in the strivings of an ascetic, and many of the interior tribulations of the saints that are reported by tradition are explained today by the strong psychological forces that are at work within us. But the fact that the boundary lines between nature and the supernatural cannot be drawn clearly—particularly in these areas—in no way contradicts the assumption that the tempter makes use of those psychological forces as well and exerts influence on them.

Just as he tempted the saintly masters in the desert, so too he stirred up in their disciple Anthony memories of his former property, his sister, his dealings with his relatives, and the many joys of life. At the same time he set before his eyes the arduousness of the life of virtue, the weakness of the flesh, and the length of the years. Yet Anthony did not allow himself to be dissuaded and fought against the temptations with prayer and faith. Anthony even saw a deeper meaning in the temptations and later taught: "No one can enter into the kingdom of heaven without being tempted. Take away the temptations, and no one is saved."

Athanasius goes on to report that the devil then set about attacking Anthony at a young man's weakest spot by confronting him with phantasms of sexual allurements. In times like ours, in which sexual allusions and images are omnipresent, one loses a sense of the connection between the spiritual life and a chaste disposition. Yet Anthony was aware that it is precisely impurity that is capable of killing a human being spiritually. When he withstood these temptations, the devil appeared to him in bodily form as a black boy and said to him in a human voice: "I have deceived many, and I have brought down a multitude, but just now I was helpless in employing against you and your efforts the same tactics I have used against others." When Anthony asked who he was, he replied with a mournful cry, "I am the friend of fornication. I am the one who has undertaken to trap young people into fornication and entice them with its blandishments. I am called 'the spirit of fornication'! How many desired to live chastely, and I led them astray! How many professed such a desire, and I enticed them to change their minds! It is I whom the prophet censures on account of those who have fallen when he says: 'You have been led astray by a spirit of harlotry' [Hos 4:12]. They have been tripped up because of me! I am the one who has harassed you so often—but just as often my plans have been wrecked by you!" [6.2–3].[1] Anthony answered the devilish figure: "You are a despicable wretch, that is what you are, for you are black of mind, and you are a frustrated child. From now on I am not going to pay any attention to you, for 'the LORD is my helper, and I shall look upon my enemies'" [6.4]. At that the impure spirit fled and troubled Anthony no more.

Anthony was aware, however, that the devil would devise a new stratagem by which to tempt him, and so he intensified his ascetical practices after this initial victory. It should be noted that the exercises of a Christian ascetic are not supposed to enable him to boast of his special accomplishments or to make a show of his special abilities. The primary purpose of asceticism is to strengthen the will and to become master of one's urges, which otherwise increasingly take control. By all means, we can call this struggle for true self-control a cultivation of the whole human being, for without it a creature endowed with reason sinks to the level of a beast. Anthony himself knew the dangers of asceticism and

---

[1] These numbers represent the paragraph and verse numbers from *The Life of Antony: The Coptic Life* and *The Greek Life*, trans. Tim Vivian and Apostolos Athanassakis (Kalamazoo, Mich.: Cistercian Publications, 2003). Used with permission.

clearly indicated that asceticism alone does not save, for instance, when he warned: "There are men who have ruined their body in striving for asceticism, and yet, for lack of the gift of discernment, have missed by far the way to God." The danger of falling into self-righteousness was even greater, which caused Anthony to say once in his later years: "I know monks who after much effort had a fall and went mad because they had placed their hope in their own work, miscalculated [their strength], and gave no thought to the prayer of the one who said, 'Ask your father, and he will show you' (Deut 32:7)."

What, specifically, did Anthony's ascetical practices consist of? How did he subdue his body? First he slept less and less, until he sometimes stayed awake the whole night. When he did sleep, then it was either on a simple mat made of rushes or else on the ground. The ascetic limited his intake of food to one meal after sundown. It could even happen that he ate only once every two to four days. His food consisted solely of bread and salt, and he drank only pure water. He renounced the Oriental custom of using oil for hair and skin care, because he said that it made the body soft. His motivation for all this was his conviction that the soul attains its greatest vigor only when the bodily cravings are powerless. In this endeavor Anthony did not reckon the time that he had already spent on the path of virtue but rather acted as though he had to begin anew each day with his ascetical practices. The example that he kept in mind was the Old Testament prophet Elijah, whose goal was to make himself the man that he was supposed to be when he appeared before God: pure of heart and ready to obey the will of God alone.

ANTHONY AMONG THE TOMBS

As he continually made progress in his ascetical way of life, Anthony sensed also a need to move farther away from his home. His journey took him first to the tombs, which were located at a great distance from the village. To this day tombs and graveyards exert a peculiar fascination. Some people are filled with an irrational fear when they think of those final resting places of the dead, whereas others feel drawn to them by a veritable longing for death. And haven't there even been saints who during their lifetimes already used coffins as their nocturnal resting places? How could Anthony make it any clearer that he had died to sin so as to live in Christ than by making a tomb his home? Our hermit asked an acquaintance to bring him bread at long intervals so that he could devote himself entirely to solitude and to advance along the steep path of perfection.

While he was living among the tombs, something happened that surpassed the earlier demonic temptations and that might incline the modern reader to relegate it to the category of legend or to ascribe a natural explanation to it: Anthony was physically attacked by a host of demons and struck to the ground. This caused the saint unspeakable pains, and he lost consciousness. Whereas many disconcerted biographers in the recent past mention the possibility that highway robbers may have attacked the hermit, we take the liberty of regarding the account by Athanasius, which relies on the firsthand testimony of the Abbot, as the unvarnished truth.

(Of course, it is not every day that purely spiritual beings manifest themselves to the senses, and it is even rarer that fallen spirits perpetrate violence in a physical way as well. And yet the more recent biographies of Saint John Vianney, better known as the Curé of Ars, or of Saint Pio of Pietrelcina teach us that such manifestations of the evil one are possible and do occur. They do not affect the average Christian and therefore should not worry the reader. Usually the ones attacked are the heroes of the Christian life who arm themselves in a special way against those powers that are not of flesh and blood.) As Divine Providence arranged it, Anthony was discovered by his acquaintance on the very next day and was carried to the village church. The villagers and his relatives were already gathering, afraid that Anthony was dead. Around midnight, however, the saint regained consciousness, while most of those around him were sleeping. He beckoned to one confidant who was keeping watch and asked him to pick him up and bring him to the tombs without awakening the others. The man did as he was told and shut the hermit—who was physically battered but spiritually strong—up in his hollowed-out tomb again.

Anthony was so weak that he could not yet even stand to pray, and so he prayed lying down. With holy defiance he then called to his demonic opponents, "Look, here I am—Anthony! I will not run from your blows! Even if you do worse things to me, nothing 'will separate me from the love of Christ'." Then he intoned the psalm verse "Though an army should array itself against me, my heart will not be afraid" [Ps 27:3]. The wicked enemy was so furious at the saint's reaction that he cried to his demonic cohorts, "You see that neither with the spirit of fornication nor with blows have we stopped this fellow. On the contrary, he stubbornly opposes us! Let us approach him some other way!" [9.2–4].

The following night, in the hollowed-out tomb, which otherwise was proverbially as silent as death, there was a likewise proverbial hellish din that caused the entire locality to tremble. And just as the devil can assume the most varied forms—anything from a snake to an angel of light—so too the demons who were attacking took on the forms of wild animals: they appeared as lions, bears, leopards, bulls, vipers, asps, scorpions, and wolves. It appeared that this multitude was about to pounce on Anthony, but they were as though tethered. The saint did feel intense bodily pain, which caused him to groan, but it in no way diminished his clarity of mind, and he scoffed at the demonic attacks: "If you had any power in you, one of you would be enough. But since the Lord has taken away your power, you attempt to terrify me any way you can by sheer numbers. Mimicking the forms of irrational beasts, as you do, only demonstrates your weakness, however. If you are able and have received authority against me, do not hesitate, but attack now. But if you are not able, why do you bother me to no purpose? Our seal and wall of protection is our faith in the Lord" [9.9–10].

The incident that day was the final test that the Lord required of his servant before he deemed him worthy of beholding his inexhaustible light. It was that light which the apostles saw for the first time on the mountain of the Transfiguration and hence has been called by the mystics "the light of Tabor". The roof of the tomb suddenly seemed to open up over Anthony, and a ray of light broke through the gloom. The demons disappeared, and the bodily pains, which moments before still caused Anthony to sigh, completely vanished. Nor did any sign of the hellish activity remain in his dwelling. Anthony took a deep breath and turned to the heavenly vision. Knowing full well the identity of the sublime guest who was appearing to him, he asked, "Where were you? Why did you not appear at the beginning so you could stop my sufferings?" The answer came in a resounding voice that was none other than the one that Moses had heard in the Burning Bush and on Mount Horeb, that voice which had spoken to many prophets and caused the Apostle Paul to fall to the ground: "Anthony, I was here, but I waited to see your struggle. And now, since you persevered and were not defeated, I will be a helper to you always and I will make you famous everywhere" [10.2–3].

At that Anthony stood up and prayed. After this encounter with God he sensed that he had more power and strength than ever before. At this point [in the *Life*] we also learn for the first time something about the age of the saint. Athanasius writes succinctly: "He was about thirty-five years old at that time" [10.4]. Although the account may have given the reader the impression that only a few months had passed since the death of his parents and his first attempts at asceticism, now it is clear that Anthony had already been traveling for fifteen years along the path to perfection.

ANTHONY GOES INTO THE DESERT

Prompted by the experiences just related, Anthony emerged from the tomb the next day and visited the aged hermit who served as his model of asceticism. He asked him to go with him into the desert and to live there. The old man, however, refused on account of his age. Besides, Anthony's plan was something new. From time immemorial the desert was considered a place of demons which was uninhabited by human beings and so hostile to life that it seemed to be abandoned even by God. Yet did not the Divine Redeemer visit the desert before beginning his public ministry, so as to arm himself by fasting and prayer, and did not Israel also have to cross the desert first before it could reach the Promised Land? What could be more obvious, therefore, than for our ascetic also to take that final step in his life of renunciation and voluntary privations and to go into the desert? Moreover, the desert gave Anthony the opportunity to concentrate on the essential battle of the ascetic. He himself explained this in one of the *apophthegmata* in these words: "He who stays in the desert solitude in impassive silence is shielded from three battles: those that come from hearing, speaking and seeing. He has only one battle left to fight: against his own impurity."

Once again the Adversary made an attempt to bring about Anthony's downfall by causing him to see along the way a mirage of a silver plate and then even some real gold. Anthony not only left the seductive treasures lying by the wayside but even started to run so as to leave these temptations behind as well. What did he care about dazzling metal when he was privileged to experience rays of heavenly light? He hastened beyond the river to Mount Pispir, on which there was an abandoned barracks, and he chose this as a suitable dwelling place.

The barracks had been abandoned for so long that it was full of vermin, which are described by Athanasius as "creeping reptiles". Yet just as Saint Patrick banished all snakes from Ireland, so the reptiles gave way to the saintly hermit Anthony. Far from all idyllic scenes, the ascetic entrenched himself in his abode. He had brought with him a half year's supply of bread, and water was available in the barracks, probably in the form of a spring. In this regard Athanasius mentions that the people of Thebes sometimes store their bread for a whole year, which could indicate a sort of zwieback. Anthony lived in complete solitude in the barracks and avoided all contact with the outside world. Only twice a year a trusted assistant came and lowered bread down to him into his self-appointed cloister. Other acquaintances who tried to visit the hermit were not allowed in. That may seem harsh to us today, especially since many of them were surely seeking the wise man's counsel. Yet Anthony was still in a process of maturing. Just as a butterfly in the pupa stage cannot be taken out of its cocoon— for then it could never arrive at the development of those aptitudes which will eventually make out of the unsightly caterpillar that splendid, multicolored butterfly that lifts itself above the earth on its wings—so too at this stage of his ascetical formation any development or maturation might have been disrupted. Furthermore, human beings in the third century had the same weaknesses as they do in the twenty-first. Thus many of Anthony's contemporaries surely were drawn to the barracks only to catch a glimpse of that

amazing man who was completely different from your average acquaintance and about whom many marvelous things
were recounted.

Those who were more serious about their visit often
waited for several days and nights outside the barracks. During that time it seemed as if they heard voices inside that
berated Anthony and tried to drive him away: "Get away
from what belongs to us! What are you doing in the desert?
You will not be able to endure our connivings!" [13.2].
And just like the enlightened man of the modern era, these
visitors also thought that someone with a ladder had climbed
into the hermit's realm so as to chase him away. Yet when
they peered through various cracks and could not see
anyone, the idea occurred to them that it might be demons.
In their fright their cried out to Anthony to help them,
for they were aware that only the saint was in a position to
deal with those powers, since only he wore, as Paul expresses
it, the armor of God (see Eph 6:13). Anthony actually came
to the door but kept it closed. He advised the visitors to go
away and to have no fear, since the demons caused phan-
toms to appear only to those who were afraid of them.
"Just make the sign of the cross and depart in peace. Let
them jeer at themselves."

Anthony, however, continued his battle against the demons,
without suffering any harm. He must have been edified more
frequently now by heavenly apparitions, which gave him
increasing strength as he grappled with his enemies. His
acquaintances, who in their need came to see Anthony again
and again, regularly found him praying the psalms.

"Let God arise, let his enemies be scattered; let those
who hate him flee before him! As smoke is driven away, so
drive them away; as wax melts before fire, let the wicked
perish before God!" (Ps 68[:1–2]). Anthony expressed his
affliction and his hope when he cited Psalm 118:10: "All

nations surrounded me; in the name of the LORD I cut them off!" He sang the psalms, which to this day are a fixed component of the Church's Divine Office and recall the saving deeds of the Almighty. Even today those same psalms are still part of the Church's ceremony of exorcism, that great prayer of liberation which is truly medicinal and strengthens the soul. And anyone who is beset by psychological distress or spiritual temptations should join in that great song of Israel's praise so as to experience consolation and healing.

THE FIRST MONASTIC
FOUNDATIONS

Anthony spent an unimaginable period of time—almost twenty years—in complete solitude, without leaving the barracks. Only when the number of those who wanted to imitate Anthony's way of life had become too large and his acquaintances broke down the door to his dwelling did Anthony come outside. It is a phenomenon in the lives of many saints that they often have to be forced by the simple people to accomplish a great mission in their lives, since they do not believe themselves capable of the task or are afraid of losing their humility. Just think of Saint Martin of Tours, who tried to avoid being elected bishop by fleeing and hiding, or of Pope Saint Celestine, who was forced to give up his life as a hermit so as to occupy the See of Peter. Something similar happened to our saint as well. Perhaps Anthony, unbeknownst to the world, would have spent the rest of his life in the seclusion of his barracks, had the people around him not been convinced that he was destined for greater things.

Yet the years of asceticism, of praising God in prayer and fighting the demons, had finally had their effect. Athanasius chooses well-considered words which nevertheless testify to Anthony's inner transformation: "Then Anthony emerged as though from some shrine, having been initiated into divine mysteries and inspired by God" [14.2].

The bystanders marveled, however, that the physical appearance of the hermit had not changed at all since his retreat into complete solitude. Neither the lack of movement, nor the fasting, nor the protracted battles had left their mark on his body. This probably has to do with the interior equilibrium and inner freedom that Anthony had attained and which immediately became evident. He was neither careworn nor exuberant, and the great crowd that had gathered to watch him did not make him nervous. The decades-long battle against evil inclinations within and the temptations from without had been won. Anthony had achieved a union with God such as is granted to only a few human beings on earth. As an instrument of the Divine Redeemer he was endowed with many charismatic gifts: he healed physical sufferings, drove out demons, comforted the sorrowing, reconciled enemies, and admonished everyone that they must not prefer any earthly thing to the love of Christ. Since he advised his listeners to keep always in mind the good things of the world to come and God's love of mankind, we are certainly not mistaken in assuming that he had not only experienced this loving kindness personally and intensely but that he had also been privileged to see those future glories already.

Immediately Anthony began recruiting for the solitary life. Who would have been better suited than Anthony to inspire others to undertake this preeminent form of following Christ? He had experienced in his own flesh and in his spirit every possible temptation and trial that one could imagine, and by the grace of God he had made it through the refining fire, so as to recruit now, with purity and integrity, for his way of life. Athanasius records no details about the monastic foundations that followed, but describes them succinctly: "And so monastic dwellings came into being in the mountains and the desert was made a city by monks. Having left their homes, they registered themselves for citizenship in heaven" [14.7]. And so they formed on Mount Pispir the first monastic settlement that goes back directly to Anthony. Here we have to be somewhat careful about using the term "monastery". The saint's foundations consisted of loose associations of monks, who nevertheless could still be described as "anchorites" or hermits living a solitary life. This was eventually replaced by the common life of cenobites by the monk Pachomius.

The term "registration" or "enlistment" selected by Athanasius alludes directly to the process of recruiting soldiers. And aren't monks soldiers of Christ also? Like the soldier, the monk leaves family and friends so as to travel abroad and face uncertainty. And doesn't the Apostle Paul call up the Christian community at Ephesus for battle (see Eph 6:10–20)? Whereas the soldier fights against a man of flesh and blood like himself, the monk contends with much greater enemies, his own inclinations and drives and the temptations of the devil's army: "For we are not contending against flesh and blood, but against the principalities, against the powers, against the world rulers of this present darkness, against the spiritual hosts of wickedness in the heavenly places" (Eph 6:12). Yet at the same time the monk knows that Christ marches ahead of him as the commander in chief, and he is acquainted with the weapons and defensive shields with which he is equipped, according to the apostle's instructions:

Therefore take the whole armor of God, that you may be able to withstand in the evil day, and having done all, to stand. Stand therefore, having fastened the belt of truth around your waist, and having put on the breastplate of righteousness, and having shod your feet with the equipment of the gospel of peace; besides all these, quench all the flaming darts of the Evil One. And take the helmet of salvation, and the sword of the Spirit, which is the word of God. Pray at all times in the Spirit, with all prayer and supplication. To that end keep alert with all perseverance, making supplication for all the saints. (Eph 6:13–18)

Although the apostle's words apply in principle to all Christian believers, nevertheless it is the monastic state that stands on the front lines in carrying out this battle. Anthony himself had fought that battle and could now train the young troops as their drill sergeant. At the same time Anthony now became the Abbas, or Abbot, the father of the monks. To this very day he is designated by this title, which, along with the names "the Great", "the Hermit", or "the Desert Father", is inseparably connected with Anthony.

The monks who joined Saint Anthony—how many they were is no longer known—had found a schoolmaster such as the world of antiquity would never again see, and they joyfully accepted the saint's admonitions and recommendations. The discernment of spirits which Anthony himself had acquired, not in a scholar's study, but rather on the battlefield, enabled him to recognize the weaknesses of each individual disciple and to prescribe the correct spiritual medicine. Athanasius is certainly exaggerating to some extent when he describes the monastic mountain as a place free of injustice and almost a paradise on earth. Yet it should not be overlooked that the disciples had to go through the same school of hard knocks from which the teacher had already graduated. They too had to withstand the interior battles of the soul and the hostility of the wicked foe. Their hardships were mitigated nevertheless by their common prayer and the wisdom of Anthony. He also made it clear, however, that probation lasts a whole lifetime, and that man is perpetually in danger of falling. And so the hermit, withdrew again and again into the solitude of his cloister and practiced asceticism.

JOURNEY TO ALEXANDRIA

It is not often noted that the very same years in which Saint Anthony was devoting himself to asceticism and spiritual training were also a time of peace for the Christian religion. As if respite had been granted to the saint so that he could then appear on the scene armed against a vastly more powerful enemy, the last Christian persecution by the Roman Empire broke out after Anthony had founded the first clusters of monks in faraway Egypt.

In the year 303, during the reign of Emperor Diocletian, the decisive battle—the last and bloodiest—between Christianity and the Roman Empire flared up. An imperial edict issued on February 23 of that unfortunate year ordered the destruction of all churches, the burning of sacred books, and a ban on Christian worship. Christian officials and employees at the imperial court were summarily dismissed, and many of them were executed on charges of arson. In the imperial residential city of Nicomedia, Bishop Anthimus was put to death along with his priests and deacons. More edicts followed, which extended the persecution to the entire clergy of the Roman Empire. Numerous men of God were arrested, tortured, and slain. In the spring of 304 the Christian laity as well became targets of the anti-Christian terror by edict: the entire population was required to sacrifice to the pagan idols and to the Caesars. Plainly the ultimate goal was to destroy Christianity completely. Whereas in the western regions of the

empire the persecution assumed moderate proportions, it
reached its highest point in the east under Augustus Gale-
rius and his Caesar Maximinus Daza in the years 305–311.
Athanasius himself mentions the latter name in his *Life of
Saint Anthony*. The number of victims and the cruelty of
the methods of execution revealed the demonic face of
paganism. Only in 311 did the persecution relent, and as
of 313, during the reign of Emperor Constantine, Christianity would even acquire the status of official state religion. The light of the Christian faith had triumphed over
the darkness of paganism!

But what was Anthony doing during this time? Did he
remain in the seclusion of his monastic cell and leave the
fighting to others? If we suspected that, then we would be
completely wrong about the hermit. He knew that he was
not fasting, praying, and doing penance for his own sake;
rather, he was performing his service for the Mystical Body
of Christ, the Church. As Blessed Rupert Mayer, a priest
from Munich, once put it, "God hates the peace of those
whom he has destined for battle", and so Anthony could
not remain in the peace of his cell, either. As soon as he
heard about the persecutions and executions of his fellow
believers, and the first condemned Christians were taken away
to Alexandria, Anthony hastened to follow them. He himself experienced a longing for martyrdom, for the opportunity to testify with his own blood. This may be almost
incomprehensible to us today. After all, the instinct for self-
preservation is the strongest drive in a human being, and
every rational person makes an effort to avoid what is dangerous to life and limb and not to surprise the lion in his
den. The ascetic's yearning is understandable only if one has
the great faith of an Anthony. His whole life already consisted of dying [to self] in Christ, and so he would have
been ready also to imitate his divine Master totally by giving

his life. Although one could not be certain about the immediate fate of an individual Christian after his death, whether he had died in a state of mortal sin and thus was to be consigned to eternal damnation, or whether he still needed a time of purification because of a certain lukewarmness, the destiny of a martyr was and is considered unambiguous. Anyone who sacrifices his life because of his love for Christ and for the Church can apply to himself the words of Jesus to the repentant thief: "Today you will be with me in Paradise" (Lk 23:43). On the Isle of Patmos the Apostle and Evangelist John was privileged to behold the destiny of those witnesses who had shed their blood: "I saw under the altar the souls of those who had been slain for the word of God and for the witness they had borne" (Rev 6:9).

Anthony realized, no doubt, that he was permitted to long for martyrdom but could not obtain it by force. So he did the best that he could under the circumstances: he served the confessors who had been sent to the mines and the prisons. He strengthened the accused when they were on trial, encouraging them and inspiring confidence. When they fearlessly gave testimony to their faith, he accompanied them to their execution. Athanasius uses here the expression "until they were perfected". The martyrs had completed their earthly course, and already the prize of victory was certainly theirs. The efforts of Anthony and his disciples did not escape the judge's notice, however, and he not only forbade the monks to appear in court but also expelled them from the city. Whereas all the other monks now went into hiding, Anthony washed his outer garment, positioned himself the following day in a prominent place, and showed himself to the presiding judge. Even as the magistrate walked by the hermit, the saint showed no fear. Instead he gave good example, as Athanasius puts it, "demonstrating the resolve of the Christians" in all its splendor.

When the great bishop and confessor of Alexandria uses these words, he is speaking to the Christians of all times and is also challenging today's reader of his words to do away with all tepidity and courageously to give witness to the faith, as the Abbot risked his life to do. We do not know how the judge in question reacted. We can merely imagine his startled expression on seeing the impudent monk. Like the enemies of Christ, he probably did not dare to proceed against Anthony. The latter's appearance had accomplished one thing, though: he was now able to serve the confessors again unimpeded. Only when the persecutions came to an end—we mentioned earlier that that must have been around the year 311—did Anthony withdraw again to his monastery on Pispir.

There he continued his interior struggle uninterruptedly and did not relent in his asceticism. He went on fasting and did not wash his body. For the first time we learn from Athanasius a more precise detail about the ascetic's clothing: the saint wore a hair shirt as an undergarment and an outer garment made of animal skins. Again and again Anthony made retreats for a time, during which he did not visit the brothers and also allowed no one to see him. This undertaking, however, seldom met with success, since the people looking for him repeatedly intruded and asked him for advice and assistance. When he then brusquely turned them away and challenged them to pray their own prayers, his motive was not a lack of charity but rather a concern that he himself could fall by pride through the deeds that God worked through him, or that he might be honored unduly by those who sought his help. At the same time he wanted to counteract the laziness of the petitioners, for instance, when a brother asked for his prayers he replied, "I have no pity on you, and God has none either, unless you yourself make the effort and ask God." Readers of saints' lives will immediately recall the stories and literary portraits of Padre Pio. This great monk and miracle worker of the twentieth century, too, not infrequently had to turn believers away with a harsh word, or even on one occasion to make room by threatening to lash out with his cincture.

INTO THE INTERIOR DESERT

In order to avoid the frequent disturbances, the saintly hermit finally decided to travel to the Upper Thebaid, where he was unknown. The monks gave him bread to take with him on the journey, and Anthony sat down on the bank of the Nile to wait for a ship that could transport him upriver. Deep in thought, he suddenly heard again the familiar voice that had first spoken to him in the rock cave. The divine voice repeated the question that it had once asked Peter, the Prince of the Apostles, outside the gates of Rome: "Anthony, where are you going, and why?" By then Anthony used to speak with the Lord as though with an intimate friend, and he answered, "Since the crowds do not allow me any peace and quiet, I want to travel to the Upper Thebaid on account of the numerous distractions taking place here, and especially because they are always asking things from me that are beyond my ability." Yet the voice from heaven replied to the wise man, "Even if you go up to the Thebaid, as you propose, even if you go downstream to Boukolia [the Pastures], you will find plenty of troubles remaining, even twice as many as you have now. But if you really desire peace and quiet, leave now for the interior desert." Anthony replied, "And who will show me the way? I have no idea how to get there" [49.2–5]. By Divine Providence he immediately saw a group of Saracens who were traveling that same route. The Saracens welcomed the hermit into their party, and he walked for three days and three nights with them into the desert, until he reached a high mountain. It was Mount Kolzim, which Anthony chose for his hermitage and which from then on became known also as Saint Anthony's mountain. Its location was described by the priest Cronius in the *Historia Lausiaca*, when he reported that Anthony "lived between Babylon and Herakleopolis, deep in the vast desert which extends toward the Red Sea, almost thirty miles distant from the river." In his account of the subsequent years Athanasius refers to the saint's retreat as the "Inner Mountain" and to the settlement of monks in Pispir as the "Outer Mountain". At the foot of the mountain there was clear, flowing water, and in the vicinity there was a plain with date palms. At first the Saracens brought bread for Anthony with their caravans. Later on some of the brothers, too, learned where the monk was staying and began to send bread to him. Anthony, however, did not want to be a burden to anyone and asked only for a two-pronged hoe, an ax, and some grain. Equipped in this way, he began to clear and cultivate a small garden by which to provide for himself. Then, when visitors began to appear again, he started a vegetable garden as well, so as to offer hospitality for his guests. In addition the saint busied himself by weaving baskets, which he gave to his benefactors in return. Wild animals damaged his crops at first, but the saint admonished them and they obeyed him. This too, incidentally, is reliably reported in many lives of the saints: someone who is so close to God is capable of exerting a special power even over irrational creatures. Just think of the *Poverello*, Saint Francis of Assisi, who proclaimed the Good News about Jesus Christ even to the birds and made the Holy Father wait for him because he had to repair a spider's web that he had inadvertently torn. When sin is overcome, then this already achieves in a fragmentary way, so to speak, the peaceful coexistence of paradise that is foretold by the prophet

Isaiah for the time of fulfillment, when the wolf and the lamb will graze together (see Is 65:25).

Anthony would not have been Anthony, the demon fighter, if his battles against the powers of darkness had not continued in the interior of the Upper Thebaid region. Here, too, visitors used to hear noise, voices, and a great din, and they would see the hermit, who by then was up in years, advancing against the infernal powers as though contending with visible opponents. Athanasius reports that the old man not only suffered demonic attacks but also experienced consolations from the divine Savior. When he disclosed to the wild animals his identity as a servant of Christ, they fled from him as the Gerasene herd of swine had done from his Master. And when the hermit once saw in a spiritual vision all the snares that the wicked foe had set throughout the world, he sighed and asked, "Who, then, can escape them?" Thereupon he heard a voice that spoke only one word: "Humility!"

ANTHONY'S MIRACLES

The many miracles that Anthony subsequently worked in the power of Christ are compiled in minute detail by Athanasius. Of course it is not possible for us to examine each one of the events as to its authenticity and plausibility. And however important it may be to the modern, critical mentality, we make no attempt at all to do so, either. Instead we want to acknowledge the possibility of miracles, which break the laws of nature as we know them. It has always been Catholic doctrine that the truth of the Christian religion can be demonstrated externally also through the fulfillment of the Old Testament prophecies and by miracles, which serve both to confirm the truth of what is proclaimed and also to signal the beginning of the Kingdom of God. The devil and his minions cannot work true miracles but are capable only of deceiving and mimicking. All of Church history is filled with the marvelous and incomprehensible works that God has performed for his children. To this day the Church requires heavenly confirmation, so to speak, in the form of several miracles that can be attributed to the intercession of the person in question, before she declares that a witness to the faith was a saint. The records of canonization processes in the archives of the Congregation for the Causes of the Saints testify to the countless confirmed healings, conversions, and wonders that have been worked in the name of Christ to the glory of God and for the salvation of souls in the two-thousand-year history of the Church. Modern exegetes of

Scripture must be blind when they ignore these testimonies and explain away the miracles of the God-man as parables and legends. Athanasius, too, is acquainted with the doubts of his contemporaries and remonstrates with them: "We cannot be unbelievers if such great miracles take place through a human being!" He cites the parable of the mustard seed and the power of Christian prayer. At the same time, he never fails to indicate that it is not Anthony's power that works miracles and that Anthony never commands, either; rather, he prayed and called on Christ, and thus the Lord himself worked them.

Anthony trusted, without doubts or worries, in God's intervention when he turned to him in prayer. And that trust is in fact what makes it possible to work miracles in the power of Jesus Christ. As long as Peter trusted it was possible for him, too, to walk on the water of the sea. If one only has faith the size of a mustard seed, the Redeemer promises that it will have miraculous power. Yet Anthony's faith had far surpassed the size of a mustard seed, since he had overcome many demonic attacks and had obtained many heavenly consolations. Why, therefore, should we not lend credence to these old accounts, when we cannot deny the miraculous events in the lives of Don Bosco, Vincent Pallotti, Padre Pio, or Sharbel Makhluf, the wonder-working monk from Lebanon?

It so happened that the hermit's disciples, who missed him very much, invited him to visit them once again in Lower Egypt. On the long journey through the desert they ran out of water, and there was a real danger that they might die of thirst. The saint walked some distance away from them, knelt down, stretched out his arms, and prayed. Immediately a spring opened up beside him, from which they were all able to drink and to fill their leathern bottles. The group was able to continue on their journey refreshed and to tell the other monks about the miraculous event. Anthony himself was welcomed as a father; after all, his spiritual sons had missed him and his advice very much. For the first time we hear again about the hermit's sister. Like her older brother, she too had chosen a life of virginity and meanwhile had become the superior of other virgins. After these meetings Anthony went back to live again on his mountain, and from then on he received visitors and people seeking counsel more often.

The instructions and admonitions that Anthony used to repeat to his visitors can be characterized as perennially valid; they already anticipate many points that are inseparably connected with the later Rule of the saintly father Benedict. First and foremost is the demand to trust God and to love him. Those seeking counsel are then admonished to guard against unclean thoughts and fleshly desires and to flee from all ambition. The ascetic knows the right medicine to prescribe against these temptations and dangers: he mentions constant prayer, the singing of psalms before going to sleep and upon awaking, meditation on the divine commands, remembering and imitating the saints. Furthermore Anthony emphasized the saying of the Apostle Paul "Do not let the sun go down on your anger" [Eph 4:26] and extended it to all sinful actions. In order to accomplish all this, a daily examination of conscience is indispensable. We must quote here verbatim some advice that is as relevant today as it was seventeen hundred years ago and allows for the fact that most evil deeds occur in secret:

> Let each of us note and write down his deeds and the movements of his soul as though we were going to report them to each other. Be assured that if we are thoroughly ashamed to have others know these things, we will stop sinning and even stop thinking altogether about doing anything evil.

What sinner wants to be seen? Who, after sinning, does not lie, wanting to escape undetected?

Therefore, just as we watch one another in order not to commit sexual sin, in the same way if we write down our thoughts as though we were going to report them to one another, we will keep ourselves very far away from filthy thoughts, ashamed as we are to have others know about them. So let this practice of writing things down take the place of our fellow ascetics' eyes so that, being as embarrassed to have our sins written down as seen, we will not think in our hearts about anything evil at all. If we form each other [or: train ourselves] this way, we will be able to make a servant of the body and please the Lord while trampling on the Enemy's deceptions. [55.9-13]

But let us return now to the miracles recorded by tradition. As he reports various healings in the next part of the *Life of Saint Anthony*, Athanasius not only is able to name the persons healed and to state precisely where they came from, but also often notes quite precisely the sorts of illnesses that they had. The proximity in time between the events and the written account rules out the possibility that these are legends meant to glorify Anthony. Thus the *Life* tells about a man named Fronto from Palation who suffered from a serious malady that caused him to gnaw at his own tongue and impaired his sight. He asked Saint Anthony for his prayers. Anthony recited the prayer for the sick and ordered him to leave the desert; then, he would be healed. At first the sick man wanted to stay with Anthony, but once he had arrived in Egypt at the hermit's behest, he was restored to health. As in many biblical healings, here there is, besides the motives of faith and trust in God Almighty, another element which is necessary for the healing: obedience. Only unselfish waiting upon the Lord's command makes healing from within possible.

One of the most impressive healings by the saint is the one that he performed for a young girl from Busiris in Tripoli. The child must have been severely deformed. Athanasius reports that the discharge from her eyes, nose, and ears became infested with maggots [58.1]; the child was completely paralyzed and "she did not have the normal use of her eyes." When the parents heard about monks who were planning to visit the saintly hermit Anthony, they joined their party in the hope that their child might be healed. The parents did not actually visit Anthony but waited outside the mountain with Bishop Paphnutius, a confessor and monk. Yet the brothers did not have to tell Anthony about the girl; by a heavenly inspiration he already knew about the child's sufferings and that she had made the journey too. He forbade the parents and child to enter his dwelling and instructed the brothers, "Go, and you will find her healed, if she has not died. This achievement is not mine so that every pitiable person will come to see me. No, this healing is the Saviour's: he works his mercy everywhere on those who call on him. As far as this girl is concerned, then, the Lord has agreed to hear her prayer; as for my involvement, the Lord has demonstrated his love for humanity by healing her of her infirmity over there" [58.4–5].

Palladius, too, in his *Historia Lausiaca*, reports eyewitness testimony to a healing that he heard from the aforementioned priest Cronius from Nitria. As a young man, Cronius was driven by spiritual anxiety to call upon the holy hermit. From him we learn also something about the "procedures" for visiting the recluse. Cronius traveled to Saint Anthony's Monastery on Mount Pispir. There visitors had to wait for Anthony until the hermit came down from his mountain. Many had to persevere for anywhere between ten and twenty days before the saint left his seclusion to receive visitors who were seeking his counsel. Cronius himself waited five days to meet the Abbot. During that time he also became acquainted with the monk Eulogius, who had agreed to care for a deformed man. For some time, however, the latter had been behaving so peevishly that Eulogius thought that he was possessed, and so he asked other ascetics, "What should I do? This cripple is driving me to despair! Should I put him out on the street? I don't dare, for I have made a vow. He is making my whole life miserable. I don't know where to turn." The ascetics immediately knew the right advice to give him and replied, "The Great One is still living, after all; go to him, and take the cripple with you in a boat. Bring him to the monastery and wait until he comes back from the desert, then present the case to him for discernment and do as he commands, for through him God will be speaking to you." The "Great One" was, of course, Anthony, and we see how it goes without saying that already during his lifetime people called him by that title. Eulogius invited his ward to get into a shepherd's boat and brought him to Anthony's monastery. Cronius himself now goes on to narrate that the saint arrived late in the evening on the following day. He went first to his confidant Makarius and asked, "Brother Makarius, have any brothers arrived?" When Makarius answered yes, Anthony asked the odd question, "Egyptians or inhabitants of Jerusalem?" This referred to a previous arrangement between the saint and his confidant. Anthony had instructed him, "If you see that the guests are not especially pious, then say 'Egyptians'. On the other hand, if they are very pious and recollected, then say, 'They come from Jerusalem.'" In the first case, with a group that probably came to the hermit more out of curiosity than for any other reason, he usually ordered Makarius to cook something for them to eat. Anthony himself then went to visit them briefly, prayed with them, and dismissed them. If they were "from Jerusalem", however, then the saint sat down to spend the whole night with them and talked with them about the salvation of their souls.

On that evening, when Makarius said that it was a mixed group of people, Anthony allowed the whole group to visit him. Before anyone had introduced himself, he called three times the name "Eulogius!" That man felt initially that he was not being addressed at all. Thereupon Anthony specified, "You're the one I mean, Eulogius, the one from Alexandria." Then when Anthony asked him what brought him to the monastery, the man replied, "He who has betrayed my name to you has also revealed to you my concern." At that the old man answered, "Yes, I know your concern, but say it in the presence of all the brothers, so that they too may learn about it." When Eulogius had presented his problem, Anthony became very serious and admonished him, "Do you want to disown him, then? The one who created him, however, does not disown him. Do you really want to do that? Then God will raise up someone better than you, who will then take care of him." After that Eulogius anxiously remained silent. Now Anthony turned to the cripple, and his words surely made the blood curdle in the veins of those who were listening. He screamed at him, "You miserable cripple; you are too wicked for heaven and earth. How long will you keep opposing God? Do you not know that Christ himself is serving you? How dare you, then, despise Christ? Didn't Eulogius assume the responsibility of caring for you, as though he were a slave?" Note well that the wickedness of the sick man lay not in his deformity but in his ingratitude and peevishness. After Anthony had thus admonished them both, the hermit turned to his other visitors, only to conclude by warning Eulogius and the deformed man once again: "Go straight home now and do not separate from one another but stay in your house as before. In a short time God will take you [from this earth].

You experienced that temptation because you are both already near the end and should be crowned soon. Follow all these instructions precisely so that the angel finds you together!" The two traveled home, and forty days later Eulogius died, and the deformed man not a full three days later.

A few weeks later Cronius arrived at the monastery in Alexandria where Eulogius had lived, and spoke with the monks there about the events that had transpired at Anthony's dwelling. He even swore on the Gospel book to the truthfulness of his account and explained, "During this whole story I acted as Anthony's interpreter, for he knows no Greek. But I understand both languages and translated for them into Greek and for him into Egyptian."

Another report testifies that our monk was endowed with supernatural gifts that enabled him to observe hidden and distant events. Christian literature offers many examples thereof, from prophecy to the ability to read souls. Here we will recall only Saint Jean-Marie Vianney or, in the twentieth century, Therese Neumann of Konnersreuth. Most mystics lived through a long period of physical suffering and chronic ill health before the aforementioned gifts appeared. In the case of an ascetic it is probably the radical, voluntary renunciation of bodily comforts that likewise leads to a keener spiritual sense. This is not the place to examine more closely the question of whether this is the development of natural human potential or involves special charismatic gifts. Even in this instance the inner cooperation of human nature and divine grace can probably never be completely sorted out, and the human intellect reaches the limits of its cognitive ability. For Athanasius these considerations would have been moot, and he had no doubt that the Lord was the one who showed Anthony what was happening at a distance.

In the case of our Desert Father, the following incident once occurred. Two men were on the way to visit Anthony when they ran out of water. One of them died, while the other lay down on the ground and was waiting likewise for death. At the same time Anthony on his mountain summoned two monks who were his guests and instructed them, "Take a jar of water, and quickly take the road to Egypt. Two brothers were on the way here, but one is already dead and the other one soon will be if you do not hurry. This was just now revealed to me while I was praying" [59.2–3]. The rescue of the man dying of thirst was successful.

The saint often foresaw the arrival of visitors days in advance and could even tell the purpose of their visit. Occasionally Anthony could also observe the purely spiritual, invisible world and thereby gained insights into the personal destiny of the human soul after death and separation from the body. He was sitting one day on the mountain and suddenly spied in the air a man who was being led upward and was welcomed by others who were overjoyed. It was simultaneously revealed to him that it was the soul of the monk Amoun, who lived in Nitria, a thirteen days' journey distant from Anthony. One can imagine the amazement of his friends when Anthony told them that the monk, with whom they were acquainted, had just died. About a month later brothers came from Nitria and were able to confirm that Amoun had died at precisely the hour when Anthony had seen his soul travel to heaven. In further visions the saint saw the fate of the human soul after death.

Like the great mystics of the sixteenth century (here we will mention only John of the Cross and Teresa of Avila), Anthony was aware of the danger that the evil foe is also capable of inducing visions. Once several brothers went to visit him; they wanted to tell him about their visions to find out whether they were genuine or of demonic origin.

En route a donkey perished. When they finally arrived, Anthony asked them, "How did he die on the way, your little donkey?" When the astonished monks asked him how he knew about it, he replied, "The demons made me see it!" With that he made it clear to the brothers that their visions were the work of demons.

Besides the saint's miraculous cures, prophecies, and visions, Anthony worked, like his divine Master, as an exorcist. His personal battle against the demons is already in this category, but he served other people as well by freeing them from demonic influence. While describing the temptations that beset Anthony we already examined Church teaching about the existence of demons. We will try to do this again now in greater depth: besides the visible world, the Almighty created an invisible world, as the great creeds of the early Church teach us. This is the world of purely spiritual beings who as persons are endowed with free will and reason. As originally created, these spiritual beings or angels were good. Since they were designed as persons with reason, it was of course possible for them also to choose to rebel against their Creator. The fact that Lucifer and his followers made this terrible decision is usually attributed to the pride and arrogance of the devil, who, contrary to his destiny, opposes his Creator: "I will not serve!" Because they are pure spirits, their thinking and willing is not limited, as is the case with man, whose understanding is subject to many circumstances, which also cause him to change his mind again and again. Hence their one-time decision against God was simultaneously a definitive decision. The world of the originally good spirits was divided into the kingdom of the angels, who just as definitively remain on God's side and are at the service of God and human beings, and the kingdom of the demons. Whereas the angels now cooperate in building up the Kingdom of God for the glory of God and the salvation of souls, Satan and his demons try to thwart this kingdom. This occurs mainly through a subtle temptation of man, to whom the evil spirit whispers again and again, "You will be like God!" [Gen 3:5]. Only in rare cases are there manifestations also, as we find so frequently in the life of Anthony. Such molestations are referred to also as demonic "obsession", since they approach the afflicted person from outside. In a few cases, however, it may reach the point of so-called possession. In this case the evil spirit takes possession of the body of the possessed person, who in the critical phases is not in control of his actions. This is not the place to examine closely the causes of demonic possession and the accompanying phenomena or the distinction that must be made between possession and psychiatric illnesses. We should note, nevertheless, that even in the recent past the Magisterium of the Church has confirmed this constant teaching and maintains the real possibility of demonic possession. Following the example of her divine-human Head, the Church makes a remedy available in the form of exorcism. According to the canon law currently in force, this sacramental may be carried out only by a priest who has the authorization of a bishop and is distinguished by his maturity, prudence, and moral uprightness. These restrictions were necessary in order to regulate this pastoral activity, which involves great responsibility, whereas in the early Church the work of exorcism was performed more freely.

Who would have been better qualified as an exorcist than the monk Anthony, who knew the wiles of the enemy, having experienced them in his own flesh? We have already seen in the case of Eulogius that Anthony could discern clearly between true possession, illnesses, and the moods of a person. He did not exorcize the crippled man who was

commended to his prayers, but only admonished him to do
something about his surly character.

Athanasius does report a rather serious case of possession. Visitors brought to Anthony a nobleman who was in
such a severely critical state that he would greedily gulp
down his own vomit and did not even notice that he was
in the presence of Anthony. The latter prayed and kept watch
beside the man throughout the night. On the next morn-
ing the possessed man began to strike Anthony forcefully.
When his companions became angry at this, Anthony calmed
them and pointed out that it was not the young man but
rather the demon who was assaulting him. Indeed, he had
commanded the demon to retreat to the arid wilderness,
and that was why it started to rage. A short time later the
evil spirit had to obey and it left the man. He returned to
his right mind and gratefully embraced Anthony. It may
have been one of the most moving scenes in the life of the
saint when the young nobleman lovingly hugged the
unwashed old man. In contrast to the numerous artistic rep-
resentations of the hermit in his cave or in battle with
demonic beasts, we unfortunately know of no image of this
incident.

ANTHONY FIGHTS AGAINST
THE ARIANS IN ALEXANDRIA

Until now we have dealt very little with the relation of Saint Anthony to the ordained clergy of the Church. We know from the story of his youth that he participated as a matter of course in the Christian mysteries, and it must be assumed that later also, as often as distance permitted him, he participated in the sacrifice of the New Covenant, the Divine Liturgy, the Eucharist. Many times problems with the Church's hierarchy are projected onto the great personages of the mystical life by critical minds that make an artificial division between ministry and charism. Yet the same Holy Spirit who confers on the ordained clergyman those very charisms which serve to build up the Mystical Body of Christ likewise bestows special gifts on the layman for the same purpose. We know of the reverent and childlike attitude of the lay brother Francis toward priests. (It is debated whether he ever received diaconal ordination.) For he, of all people, who by the grace of God was conformed even to the outward appearance of Christ by his stigmata, was aware that every ordained priest acts in Christ's stead and that only he, in the person of Christ, can make present the bloody sacrifice of Golgotha in an unbloody manner. So Francis admonished his confreres again in his testament to show reverence and obedience toward priests.

We learn nothing different about Anthony. He respected and observed the laws of the Church, and if he was already humble in approaching every individual who visited him, then he certainly knew how to show special respect toward the clergy. He used to bow before the bishops and priests who called on him, and whenever he happened to be in conversation with a deacon, he immediately allowed him to lead the prayers. Though far removed from any idle curiosity, the saint, wanted to be informed about goings-on in the world, and he asked his visitors about this and that.

And what impression, now, did Anthony make on his visitors? Although in his outward appearance he was essentially no different from the other monks, even visitors who were unacquainted with him were drawn to him the moment they saw him. They were attracted, as Athanasius describes it (who after all had had the privilege of seeing the hermit), by his eyes. Those aged eyes of Anthony radiated a gladness and peace that conveyed an external impression of the purity and integrity of his soul. The countenance proves to be the mirror of the soul!

We have deliberately placed these reflections about the hermit's relation to clerics and about the impression that he made on strangers who visited at the head of this chapter. For we learn here something about the saint's personality that was extremely important in his conflict with the Arians, which we will try to recount in the following pages. The peace that the saint had attained by decades of disciplining his own urges and needs and by ceaseless prayer proves that the now aged hermit surely did not allow himself to be drawn into pointless controversies about insignificant things. Yet when it was a question of maintaining the purity of the Catholic faith and he perceived the danger of falling away into heresy, then he could be a relentless fighter. Already in his early years he had learned that Satan is above all else the "father of lies" (Jn 8:44), and he knew the destructive power of heresy. That, after all, is what kills God in the hearts of men and leads them along the way to perdition. Like the Apostle Peter, Anthony warned against false teachers and their doings (2 Pet 2). He himself maintained no fellowship with schismatics or heretics (Athanasius mentions the Meletians and the Manichaeans by name), since he believed that even converse with them was harmful and endangered the soul. He spoke in a friendly manner with apostates only when he admonished them to return to true piety, in other words, to orthodoxy.

Anthony particularly despised the heresy of the Arians and forbade his disciples to go near the heretics or to embrace their bad faith. In the many visions that he had while deep in mystical contemplation, not only did he become aware of the events that were going on right then in Egypt but he also received prophetic messages concerning the future fate of Christ's Church. Similar experiences are reported about Saint John Bosco, Blessed Anne Catherine Emmerich, or the children of Fatima. The most serious vision of Saint Anthony concerned the appearance of the Arians on the world scene. After an hour-long vision that left the hermit sighing and trembling, he knelt down first and prayed. Then he stood up and wept. Surely his disciples were profoundly disturbed by the fact that a vision had cast their father down into such mourning. They had to persuade him to tell them something about what he had seen. The old man began with the words, "Children, it would be better for me to die before the events in my vision take place!" When they kept insisting, he continued amid tears, "Wrath is about to seize hold of the Church and she is about to be handed over to people who are like irrational animals. For I saw the altar of the Church and all around her mules were standing in a circle, kicking those who were inside, just like the

kicking that stampeding animals make leaping about. Surely
you heard how I was groaning! For I heard a voice saying,
'They will make an abomination of my altar'" [82.6–7].

To his great dismay, Athanasius had to experience the
uprising of Arianism against the Church two years after
Anthony's vision, just as the hermit had seen it. As in the
sixteenth century during the time of the so-called Reformation, churches were plundered and the sacred vessels were
taken away by force and carried off through the fields. Upon
the remaining altars they no longer offered the unbloody
sacrifice of Christ, but instead celebrated whatever came
into their minds. At the same time, however, Anthony con-
soled his disciples as well.

> Do not lose heart, children, for just as the Lord has been
> angry, so will he again heal. The Church will once again
> regain its proper order and shine forth as she is accustomed
> to do. You will see those who were persecuted restored to
> their rightful places, and the godless will withdraw once
> again to their lairs. You will see the faith of the faithful
> spoken with complete freedom everywhere. Only, do not
> defile yourselves with the Arians! For this teaching comes
> not from the apostles but from the demons and their father
> the Devil. Moreover, this teaching is irrational and sterile
> and comes from unorthodox thinking, just as mules are
> irrational. [82.11–13]

Now when the Arians came once to visit Anthony, he
examined their ideas and finally drove them from his mountain, declaring to them that their talk was worse than snake
venom. With that he demonstrated that he was more pru-
dent and educated than many bishops of his day who were
infected by Arian ideas.

But what were these controversies about in the first place?
Arianism is considered the final and most dangerous heresy

pertaining to the Most Holy Trinity, more specifically to the relation between the Father and the Son. Arius, the father of this heresy, was born in Libya in 260 and is thought to have been the disciple of [Saint] Lucian of Antioch. Around the year 306 he was already involved in the schism of Meletius but was reconciled again with the Church and ordained a priest in Alexandria. From around 315 on he presented his heretical views openly and thus gave rise to Arianism, which is named after him. Whereas the Church, in her profession of faith in the Trinity, teaches that the Son proceeds from the Father before all time and is, just like the Holy Spirit, "consubstantial", or one in essence with the Father and is therefore likewise God; Arius taught that the Son did come to be before all time yet is not equal to the Father. For Arius, the Son is a creature created from nothing, whose existence has a beginning and which accordingly is changeable. With that, however, God's self-revelation as a triune God is shaken to its very foundations, and the ineffable mystery, that one Divine Being exists in three Persons, is dissolved. The consequences would be that the Son in fact is not essentially true God, but at best godly, just as man can become godly through adoption. That would make the Incarnation null and void as well; in other words, God himself would not have become man but rather would have sent his highest creature. Thus Arianism posed a greater danger for the Church than the Diocletian persecutions. It is difficult to chronicle in this context the condemnations and rehabilitations of Arius, which go together with the repeated banishment of Athanasius, which was mentioned at the beginning of this book, nor is it that important for our purpose of describing Saint Anthony's appearance against the Arian heresy. We limit ourselves to mentioning that Bishop Alexandros of Alexandria had already condemned Arius and his teachings at a synod attended by around one hundred bishops. Yet Arius, too, found many bishops who stood by him and supported him. Even the rejection of the Arian heresy at the ecumenical Council of Nicaea (325) did not bring about a definitive victory over Arianism. Arius himself died suddenly in the year 336 on the day before his reconciliation at the emperor's command. Decades of controversy ensued, but his teaching was not vanquished until the Council of Constantinople (381), whereas it continued to be influential for an even longer time, for example, among the Germanic tribes. The greatest, most beautiful profession of the Church's faith in the consubstantiality of the Father and the Son is found already in the Nicene Creed, when it says about the Son, "God from God, Light from Light, true God from true God, begotten, not made, consubstantial with the Father".

Now our Anthony, of all people, who had never completed a course of studies and rejected worldly wisdom, was drawn into these controversies. The man of God was generally considered as an authority, in questions of faith as well. Therefore the Arians spread the lie that Anthony thought just as they did. That prompted the bishops and his confreres to summon Anthony to Alexandria. The monk did not require much urging, since he knew how much was at stake, and he traveled immediately to Alexandria. There, however, he condemned the Arians and declared Arianism to be the final heresy and a forerunner of the Antichrist. Furthermore he instructed the people that the Son is not a creature and that consequently he was not created out of nothing. Rather, the Word and Divine Wisdom were eternally of the same essence as the Father, which is why it would be impious to maintain that there was a time in which the Son did not exist, since he was indeed always equal with the Father. As he had warned his disciples, so too he ordered the people to have no fellowship with those

who had fallen away from the true faith, since in their super-
stition they were no different from the pagans who serve a
creature instead of the Creator. "Believe, therefore, that all
creation is angry at them because they number the Creator
and Lord of all, through whom all things came into being,
among those that came into being" [69.6].

The hermit put his God-given authority to the test here
as well by driving out demons, healing illnesses, and converting many citizens of Alexandria to the Catholic faith.
In this passage of his *Life* we learn also that Athanasius himself was present and that he was probably the one who had
Anthony summoned. Indeed, he speaks about accompanying him with the other monks when they left Alexandria.
For Anthony withdrew again into solitude on his mountain.

ANTHONY DISPUTES WITH PAGAN PHILOSOPHERS—THE EMPEROR, SOLDIERS, AND SIMPLE PEOPLE SEEK HIS COUNSEL

Already during the controversy with the Arians there were flashes of that wisdom and acumen which the old hermit had not acquired through studying books, except Sacred Scripture, nor through disputations with the learned men of the world; they were evidence, rather, of a clear and orderly mind that understood, like no other, how to concentrate and thus to go to the heart of the matter. Hence many a pagan philosopher, traveled to meet this uneducated but learned man, in order to debate with him. We read for instance about two men who came to the Outer Mountain with this intention. It is mentioned at the outset that Anthony had an interpreter, a monk who translated what was said, since he himself probably could speak Coptic only. This interpreter asked on behalf of the saint, "Why do you trouble yourselves, philosophers, coming to see such a foolish person?" When they answered that he was not foolish but rather extremely wise, they received this answer: "If you came to see a foolish person, your efforts have been wasted, but if you think I am wise, become like me, for we ought to imitate what is good. Also, if I had come to see you, I would have emulated you. But since you have come to see me, become like me: I am a Christian" [72.3–5]. We can still imagine today the dumbfounded expressions on the philosophers' faces when they were beaten with their own logic. The old man may have seen them off with a cunning smile as they went back to their learned houses.

Many of the supposedly learned also tried to have some fun by mocking Anthony for his inability to write. Anthony, however, abruptly asked his visitors, "What do you think? Which is first, the mind or letters? And which is the cause of which? Is the mind the source of letters, or are letters the source of the mind?" They correctly answered that the mind is first and that it is also the inventor of letters. To this the hermit merely replied, "The person whose mind is sound, therefore, has no need of letters" [73.1–3]. Once again dumbfounded philosophers left that place and marveled at the wisdom of that simple man. Athanasius comments on the situation in these words: "Yet his character was not wild like someone who had grown old there in the mountains; instead, he had considerable grace, like someone from the city, and his speech was seasoned with divine salt" [73.4].

When several pagan wise men came to Anthony to be informed about the Christian faith and started to ridicule faith in the cross, the man of God reacted with great severity. His response, as the interpreter translated it for the pagans and Athanasius wrote it down for posterity, is worth reprinting here in its entirety:

Which is more becoming, to confess a cross, or to attribute to those whom you call gods adulteries and the corrupting of boys? The cross of which we speak is a sign of courage and proof that we look upon death with contempt, while the things you speak of are licentious passions. Is it better, then, to say that the Word of God did not err but, on the contrary, staying as he was, for our benefit and salvation assumed a human body so that, having participated in human nature, he might make us humans participate in the divine and spiritual nature? Or is it better to liken God to irrational beings and, as a result, worship four-legged beasts and reptiles and images of human beings? For these are the objects of worship of wise men like yourselves!

How dare you ridicule us for saying that Christ appeared as a human being when you define the soul as coming from Mind and maintain that it has strayed and fallen from the vault of heaven into a body? I wish that it had changed and fallen only into human bodies, and not into four-legged beasts and reptiles! Our faith declares that the coming of Christ is for the salvation of human beings, while you propound errors about the soul being uncreated. We also know Providence's power and love for humankind: the coming of Christ was not impossible for God. You, on the other hand, in calling the soul an image of Mind, attribute to it a fall and make up myths about its mutability, and finally you introduce the idea that Mind itself is mutable because of the soul. For it is necessary that whatever form the image took be the same as that of which it is the image. When you believe such things about Mind, understand that you are also blaspheming the Father of the Mind.

Now concerning the cross, which would you say is better: to endure the cross when some plot is hatched by evil people and not to shrink from an engineered death, however it comes; or to make up false myths concerning Osiris and Isis and the plots of Typhon and the flight of Kronos and the swallowing of children and murdering of fathers? How can you sneer at the cross and not be astonished at the resurrection? Those who spoke about the one wrote about the other. Or why, since you bring up the cross, are you silent about the dead that were raised and the blind who regained their sight and the paralytics who were healed and the lepers who were cleansed and walking upon the sea and the other signs and wonders that show that Christ is not only human but also God? It is clear to me that you are doing yourselves harm by not sincerely acquainting yourselves with our Scriptures. But acquaint yourselves with them and see that the things Christ did demonstrate that he is God, who dwelt among us for the salvation of humankind.

You yourselves, then, tell us *your* beliefs. What do you have to say about irrational beasts except something irrational and brutish? But even if, as I hear, you wish to say that these things are told by you as myths and that you allegorize the rape of Korê as representing the earth and the lameness of Hephaestus as fire and Hera the air and Apollo the sun and Artemis the moon and Poseidon the sea—nevertheless, you still do not worship God. You serve the creation rather than God who created all things! If you have composed myths of this sort because creation is good, even so you were only supposed to marvel at what came into being, not turn what you made up into gods so that you would not attribute to the things that came into being the honor due the [Demiurge]. Otherwise, it is time for you to transfer the honor due the architect to the house made by him, or that of the general to the soldier. Now, then, what do you say to these things, so we may know whether the cross deserves any of your mockery? [74.3–76.4]

The pagan philosophers turned to and fro in their embarrassment and could not give Anthony an answer. He, however, smiled and continued:

These beliefs of yours are self-evidently refuted. Since you rely so heavily on argumentation with words, and since you do possess this skill, you want us too not to worship God unless we do so with argumentative speech. But first tell me this: How is reality accurately discerned, and especially the knowledge of God? Through argumentation with words, or through the working of faith? And which is more important? The working of faith, or argumentation with words? [77.1–3]

The philosophers then agreed that faith which is expressed in action has priority, and that this knowledge is certain. Anthony followed this with an instruction about faith which could be used even today as a reply to any opponent of the Christian faith:

> You have spoken well, for faith comes from the disposition of the soul whereas dialectic is a skill that belongs to those who practice it. Therefore, those in whom faith is actively working have no need of argumentation with words; in fact, it is probably superfluous. Indeed, what we know through faith, you attempt to construct with words; and often you are unable to perceive what we know. As a result, the working of faith is better and more secure than all your sophistries and syllogizings.
>
> We Christians, therefore, do not possess the mystery through the wisdom of Greek words but through the power of faith supplied to us by God through Jesus Christ. And so you will know that what I am saying is true, look now: although we do not know how to write, we believe in God, recognizing through his works his universal providence. And that our faith works, look now: we depend on our faith in Christ while you wage war with sophistries; and while your idols and delusionary practices have got you nowhere, our faith is spreading everywhere. You people, with all your syllogisms and sophistries, are not persuading us to convert from Christianity to paganism; we, on the other hand, teaching faith in Christ, are stripping you of your superstitions, with everyone recognizing that Christ is God and the Son of God. You, with all your fine and fancy words, do not hinder the teaching of Christ; we, on the other hand, invoking the name of Christ crucified, are putting to flight all the demons, whom you fear as gods. Wherever one sees the sign of the cross, magic loses its power and sorcery has no effect.

So tell us, where are your oracles now? Where are the incantations of the Egyptians? Where are the illusions of the magicians? When did all these things lose their power and come to an end except at the time when the cross of Christ appeared? Does this cross deserve ridicule then? Or, on the contrary, those things that have been nullified by the cross and refuted as powerless? Indeed, this fact is also astonishing: your beliefs have never been persecuted; instead, they are honored by people in every city. The followers of Christ, however, are persecuted, and yet our religion blossoms and flourishes more than yours. What is more, your religion, celebrated and protected on all sides, is falling into ruin, whereas the faith and teaching of Christ, ridiculed by you and often persecuted by emperors, has filled the whole world! When has the knowledge of God ever shone so brilliantly? Or when has chastity and the virtue of virginity appeared so clearly? Or when has death been looked on with such contempt except at the time when the cross of Christ appeared? No one doubts this when he sees the martyrs despising death for Christ's sake, when he sees the virgins of the Church keeping their bodies pure and undefiled for Christ.

These signs suffice to demonstrate that faith in Christ is the only true worship of God. But if still you do not believe, seeking logical proofs through words, we will not offer proof by means of "plausible Greek wisdom", as our teacher said [cf. 1 Cor 2:4], but will persuade by means of the faith that is clearly outpacing your wordy fabrications. [77.4–80.1]

Now Anthony presented to his learned visitors several possessed men who had come to him to be healed, and he challenged them as once the prophet Elijah challenged the priests of Baal (see 1 Kings 18): "Look, there are here some suffering from demons. . . . You philosophers, with your logical proofs, or by whatever skill or magic you wish, calling upon your idols, cleanse these people! If you cannot, stop waging war against us, and you will see the power of the cross of Christ!" [80.2–3].

At that the hermit called on Christ and made the sign of the cross three times over those who were suffering. The demons were driven out, and the afflicted men were healed and gave thanks to God. The philosophers, however, were alarmed and astonished at Anthony's wisdom and might. He, though, continued his instruction:

> Why are you astonished at this? It is not we who do this. It is Christ who does these things for those who believe in him. So believe yourselves. Become like us and you will see that it is not skill with words that is achieving the things we do but rather faith working through the love of Christ. If you too have this faith, you will no longer seek demonstrations through words, but will realize that faith in Christ is enough. [80.6]

There was nothing left for the visitors to do than to embrace the old man gratefully and to confess that they had been very much edified by him. We do not know whether they converted to the Christian faith after this encounter with the man of God and the miracles that they had witnessed. We can assume at least that they no longer opposed the cross publicly and certainly no longer dared to mock the faith of the Christians.

Not only the wise men of his time turned to Anthony for advice, but also the mighty and those in authority. The phenomenon is similar to what we know about the story of Diogenes or about Saint Nicholas of Flüe. Both men lived far from the world and surely were not concerned about the politics of the day. Yet precisely because they were not burdened by the cares of everyday living, the rulers believed that they offered better counsel than their own officials. Thus Emperor Constantine himself had heard about the wise hermit in Egypt and, together with his sons Constantius and Constans, sent him a letter. (We know nothing about its exact contents.) Like Diogenes, who at first was merely bothered by the fact that the emperor was standing in his sunlight, Anthony did not attach any special importance to the imperial missive. We can imagine the excitement in the rest of the monastic community over the fact that their abbot had received a letter from the imperial family. Thereupon Anthony called the monks together and instructed them, at the same time reprimanding and warning them: "Why are you so amazed that the emperor writes to us? He is human, too. Instead, be more amazed that God has written the Law for human beings and has spoken to us through his own Son" [81.3]. Only when his monks insisted did he finally say that he was willing to accept the letters, have them read aloud, and reply to the emperor. His disciples pointed out that the emperor, after all, was a Christian and that he might take offense that Anthony held him in little esteem. As a good abbot hears and heeds the advice of his disciples too, Anthony replied to the emperor and his sons. He praised them for their Christian faith but did not neglect to advise them not to consider the goods of this present world as something great, but rather to think of the judgment to come. At the same time he impressed on their minds the fact that Christ alone is the true, eternal emperor. He admonished the rulers to be humane and to provide for justice and the poor. The emperors, however, according to Athanasius' sources, are said to have been very happy with the hermit's reply.

Whereas in his youth Anthony had admired all the old hermits who had distinguished themselves with great charismatic gifts, now he himself had taken their place; indeed, he united in himself all the greatness that he had seen in the others. He admonished and warned his visitors and brusquely but mercifully held up their weaknesses for them to see. He had such great sympathy with those who had been mistreated that, as Athanasius put it, one might take Anthony himself for the one who was suffering. Many who sought advice left the hermit as though transformed, and many a man had a real conversion and became a monk. Most importantly, Anthony performed the seven spiritual works of mercy. Athanasius eloquently writes:

> In short, Antony was like a physician given by God to Egypt, for who ever went to him sad at heart and did not come back rejoicing? Who ever went mourning his loved ones who had died and did not right away lay aside his grief? Who ever went angry and did not have his anger changed to friendship? What poor person in his despair went to meet him and when he heard and saw him did not come away despising wealth and comforted in his poverty? ... Who ever came to him tempted by a demon and did not find relief? And who ever came to him troubled in his thoughts and did not have his mind calmed? [87.3–5]

In particular the saint had the gift of discerning spirits like no other. To this day such discernment is indispensable for the life of Christians and of the Church. Drawing on his own abundant treasury of experience, Anthony counseled all who were tormented by doubts, pointing out to them the associated working of the demon and teaching them how they should deal with his snares. According to the reports by Athanasius, people seeking counsel came to Egypt even from foreign lands, and all left the hermit with new strength.

Nevertheless—or rather, precisely because of this charitable activity, which brought such abundant blessings—the hermit was drawn again and again to seclusion. He had to flee the crowd, as even the Divine Redeemer did, so as to regain his strength, humanly speaking, and to be completely united with his Father. Once when he was called down from the mountain, this time by a general, Anthony explained the necessity of solitude for a monk in these words: "Just as fish die if they stay too long on dry land, monks also grow feeble if they stay too long with you and loiter among you. Like fish hurrying to the sea, therefore, we too must hurry back to the mountain or we will stay too long and forget what is within [i.e., the interior life]" [85.3–4].

THE END OF ANTHONY'S LIFE

By this time 356 years had passed since the Divine Redeemer
had taken our nature so as to free the human race from
Satan's power. One hundred and five years earlier Anthony
first saw the light of day as a Coptic boy in the insignificant
little village of Koma. He had experienced his calling almost
eighty-five years ago, and seventy years ago he had retreated
to the barracks on Mount Pispir. Already fifty years had
passed since the first monastic settlements were founded in
the desert. Two severe persecutions of Christians and the
heretical attacks of the Arians took place during the lifetime of Saint Anthony. But now this life was to approach
its final destination.

As Anthony's earthly course drew near to its conclusion, he visited his brethren, as was his custom. He had
already been prepared by Divine Providence for the end
of his life, and he spoke with great composure to the other
monks: "This is my last visit with you. I will be surprised
if we see each other again in this life. It is now time for
me to die, for I am approaching the age of a hundred and
five" [89.2–3].

At that the monks burst into tears and embraced and
kissed their spiritual father and master. Anthony himself,
however, only rejoiced that he was finally about to arrive
in his heavenly homeland. He admonished his brothers not
to become lax in their asceticism, to keep their souls free
from impure thoughts and thus to live as though they might

die any day. He enjoined them to imitate the saints and to have no fellowship with the Meletians and the Arians.

> Indeed, their godlessness is perfectly clear to everyone. If you see judges acting as their champions, do not be upset, for their perishable and short-lived delusion will come to an end. You who are pure, therefore, take special care to keep yourselves away from them and preserve the tradition of the fathers and, above all, keep a pure faith in our Lord Jesus Christ, which you have learned from the Scriptures and have often had recalled to you by me. [89.4–6]

Then the monks asked their father to spend the last days of his life with them and to die in their company. Anthony refused, however, since the Egyptians still kept their old custom of wrapping the bodies of holy men and martyrs in burial cloths and performing funeral ceremonies but not burying the bodies, placing them instead on couches in their houses so as to honor them. In the past Anthony had often advised the bishops to dissuade the people from this custom, since the body of someone who had died belongs in a grave, just as the bodies of the Old Testament patriarchs and prophets, and even the body of our Redeemer, were laid in the grave. He himself regarded the Egyptian custom as contrary to the law and wanted to make sure that he was not treated in that way. So he bade farewell to his brothers on the Outer Mountain and traveled, together with his two trusted attendants who cared for him in his old age, back to the Inner Mountain. The names of the two attendants, Makarius and Amatas, are noted in another passage. Several months later, when Anthony fell sick and sensed that death was near, he summoned these two and instructed them once again, as a spiritual testament, about everything that they should observe. He said:

As it is written, I am going the way of the fathers, for I see myself being called by the Lord. But as for you, be diligent and sober, and do not abandon the ascetic way of life that you have followed for so many years but, as though you were just now starting out, work hard at maintaining your zeal. You know that the demons are always hatching plots. You know how savage they are. But they are really weak and powerless. Therefore do not fear them but instead draw inspiration from Christ and believe in him. And live as though you were going to die each day, attentively observing yourselves, and remember the exhortations you have heard from me. Let there be no fellowship between you and schismatics and absolutely no fellowship with those Arian heretics. You know how I too have stayed away from them because they wage war with Christ and because of their heretical beliefs. Make every effort yourselves always to be united, especially with the Lord, and then with the saints, so that after your death they will receive you into the eternal habitations as friends and companions.

Think about these things yourselves, and reflect on them, and if you care about me and keep my memory as you would a father's, do not allow anyone to take my body to Egypt lest they keep it in their homes. Indeed, it was on account of this practice that I returned to the mountain and came here. You know how I have always put to shame those who do this and how I have ordered them to stop practices of this sort. Therefore you yourselves bury me and hide my body under the earth and follow my instructions so that no one knows the burial site except you alone. I will receive my body back imperishable from the Lord at the resurrection of the dead. Distribute my clothing. To Bishop Athanasius give the one sheepskin coat and the tunic I used for bedding. He gave it to me new, but I have worn it out. To Bishop Serapion give the other sheepskin coat and you keep the hair shirt yourselves. And now, God keep you, children. Antony is about to leave this life and will no longer be with you. [91.2–9]

After he embraced his companions one last time, his face again showed that cheerful serenity that was characteristic of him throughout his lifetime. Now, though, his heavenly friends were coming to meet Anthony and gladdened his heart. The battle that the saint had waged for more than eighty years against the human and demonic enemies of Christ and of the Church was over. All the temptations and challenges were over, and the crown of victory had been won. The daily dying in Christ was over, and the gates of heaven were opening for the Star of the Desert, the Abbot, the consoler of men and combatant of demons: Anthony. Just as the Little Flower, Thérèse of Lisieux, promised her friends that she could intercede more powerfully for them from heaven and would shower the earth with graces and roses, so too [more than] 1,650 years ago Anthony entered into heavenly glory as a powerful intercessor.

His two friends, however, paid their last respects to his mortal remains, wrapped them in winding sheets, and buried them, as they had promised the saint, in the ground at an unknown place. Those whom Anthony had named heirs of his meager estate—he really owned nothing more than what he wore—received the sheepskins and the cloak. In Athanasius' own words: "Those who received the sheepskin coat from blessed Antony and the worn-out cloak from him keep them and treat them as great valuables. For even seeing these things is like laying eyes on Antony, and putting them on is like bearing his admonitions with joy" [92.3].

EULOGY BY ATHANASIUS

We wish to conclude this account of Anthony's life with the words of Athanasius, which not only eulogize the saint but also present a "tribute to monasticism", for which the life of Anthony constitutes an exemplary foundation:

> This, then, was the end of Antony's life in the body and these were the principles of his ascetic discipline. Even if these things I have narrated are slight compared with that man's virtue, nevertheless consider for yourselves what kind of person was this Antony, the man of God. From the time he was a youth until great old age he kept the same zeal for ascetic discipline. He neither yielded to the desire for extravagant foods on account of old age, nor on account of his body's frailty did he change the way he dressed or ever wash his feet with water. Yet, although he persevered in these practices, no harm came to him. Indeed, maintaining even undiminished eyesight and with perfectly healthy eyes, he had good vision. Not one of his teeth fell out, though they had been worn down beneath the gums on account of the old man's advanced age. His feet and his hands also remained healthy. In short, he appeared more radiant, stronger, and more energetic than all those people who enjoy a wide variety of foods and baths and different types of clothing.
>
> This is a sign of his virtue and of his soul beloved by God: his fame spread everywhere, and everyone who saw him marveled at him, and even those who had never seen

him longed to be near him. Antony was known and recognized neither through written works nor through pro-
fane wisdom nor on account of any particular skill, but only
through his love of God. No one would deny that this was
a gift from God. For how was he heard about in Spain or
in Gaul, how was he heard about in Rome and in Africa
while he sat hidden on a mountain, except that God, who
makes known everywhere those who belong to him, from
the beginning promised also to make Antony known? For
even if these people work in secret, even if they wish to
remain unknown, the Lord reveals them to everyone, like a
lamp, so those who hear may also in the same way know
that it is possible to carry out the commandments and may
receive zeal for the road to virtue. [93.1–5]

VENERATION OF THE SAINT

Veneration of Saint Anthony, which was immense even during his lifetime, not only continued after his death but extended throughout the entire Christian world. Responsible for this were, on the one hand, Anthony's disciples and other monks who had joined this movement and had had the example of the great hermit impressed on their minds. And on the other hand there was the description of his life by Athanasius, along with the sources cited at the beginning of this book, which made our saint widely known far beyond Egypt. From antiquity the Church has celebrated the memorial of the Father of Monks on January 17, and with the exception of the Armenians, who commemorate the saint on January 18, even the separated Christian communities have kept this date. Many emblems are associated with Anthony. Again and again he is depicted together with ugly devilish figures, which symbolize his battles with the demons. Especially in the churches of the East he appears wearing the Coptic monastic habit, which is distinguished by a cowl with a gold seam. Moreover he is shown with a staff with one or two little bells on it that are to be interpreted as beggar's bells; they, like the torch or fire, are associated with the Antonite Order, which we will examine more closely. Besides the staff and bell, the pig is the most common emblem of the saint. Although it has often been interpreted as a symbol for his temptations, this impression should be corrected. The pig always accompanies the saint like a little dog and often looks up at him trustingly. This emblem probably came about because Saint Anthony soon became the patron saint of domestic animals and especially of swine. Furthermore to him was assigned patronage of swineherds, brush-, basket-, and glove-makers, knights, weavers, butchers, confectioners, farmers, and gravediggers. His intercession is sought particularly against conflagrations and in cases of erysipelas, ulcers, skin diseases, leprosy, plague, syphilis, and diseases of cattle.

ANTHONY'S GRAVE AND
THE ANTONITE ORDER

With regard to Anthony's grave, two seemingly contradic-
tory traditions exist today. The monks of Saint Anthony's
Monastery insist to this day that the grave of their saintly
father, Anthony, has never been found. No ordinary mortal
could possibly learn where the father of monasticism is resting and awaiting the resurrection of the dead. Of course,
many a tour guide is said to be willing, in return for an
ample baksheesh, to lead pilgrims to a grave in which the
saint is supposedly buried, but there is in fact no generally
acknowledged place of veneration.

This understanding seems to contradict the tradition that
in the year 561 the bones of the saint were discovered in a
miraculous manner. On the basis of the clues, the discov-
ery of the grave can be considered altogether plausible. The
relics were solemnly unearthed and brought to Alexandria.
After the conquest of Egypt by the Saracens the saint's bones
were taken in the year 635 to Constantinople. Now around
980, the story goes, the emperor of the Byzantine Empire
then reigning in Constantinople—probably Basileios II, who
has gone down in history as the Bulgarian Killer—presented
the Abbot's relics to the French count Jocelin as a gift. So
they arrived in the Diocese of Vienne in the Dauphiné [a
former province in southeastern France], where they were
laid to rest in the Church of Saint-Didier-de-la-Motte in
Motte-aux-Bois, which today bears the name of Saint

Anthony. The church was enlarged especially for the pilgrims who were expected, and Benedictines from Montmajour Abbey were placed in charge of the shrine. A great stream of pilgrims did in fact commence, which attests to the popularity of the Father of Monks.

Among those making the pilgrimage were the young knight Guérin and his father, Gaston. Guérin suffered from an epidemic inflammatory condition, which because of the subsequent events was named "Saint Anthony's fire". Modern medicine identifies it as a fungal infection caused by ergot. After the son had prayed for healing through Anthony's intercession, he and his father made a vow that if the healing occurred they would dedicate their lives and their wealth to the service of the sick. So at first a fraternity of Saint Anthony came about. From this fraternity developed the Order of Antonites, which was approved in 1095 by Pope Urban II at the Council of Clermont. Honorius III gave the members permission in 1218 to take monastic vows, and Pope Boniface VIII approved the order in 1298 as a community of monks under a Rule who prayed the Divine Office in choir. In the following years the Antonites founded several hundred hospitals, which treated Saint Anthony's fire in particular. Moreover the order possessed the privilege of attending to the Pope. Alongside the order of choir monks, Albrecht I of Bavaria founded a knightly Order of Antonites in 1382.

On January 9, 1491, the saint's relics were transferred for the last time to the parish church of Saint Julien in Arles in Southern France, where to this day they are preserved in a glass casket and venerated by the public.

Thanks to the salutary work of the Antonites, devotion to Saint Anthony flourished in the fourteenth and fifteenth centuries, especially since the Antonites made their patron saint known as they traveled around collecting alms.

During that time many churches were placed under Anthony's patronage in honor of the hermit, and they remain so today. The work of the Antonite Order ended in Germany as a direct result of the so-called Reformation. During the Baroque period the order disappeared almost completely, since cases of Saint Anthony's fire had become very rare. The remnants of the order merged in 1777 with the Order of Malta.

THE ORIGINAL HERMIT—
PAUL OF THEBES

Around twenty years after it was produced, the *Life of Anthony* by Saint Athanasius had some unexpected competition. The great Christian writer and Bible translator Jerome (347– or 348–420)—we will hear more about him in the following pages—composed between 375 and 378 his *Vita Pauli primi eremitae*, his *Life of Saint Paul, the First Hermit*. Jerome happened to be on a pilgrimage to Jerusalem and was staying in the little village of Maronia east of Antioch. Already in his foreword Jerome refers to the traditions about Anthony and candidly admits that Saint Anthony had the greatest influence on the numerous imitators who followed him in the eremitical life. Yet for Jerome the fact still remains that Anthony was not the first to live in the desert as a hermit: Paul of Thebes had had that distinction. To his sorrow he had to state that the traditions concerning Paul were very scant and that some of them were so grotesque that they could not be true, for instance, the report that Paul's hair had grown down to his heels. In order to counteract these legends and hand on the credible traditions about Paul, Jerome wrote his *Life* [*of Saint Paul, the First Hermit*], which with its eighteen chapters is notably shorter than the one by Athanasius.

Jerome begins with a short description of the Decian persecutions. During that time Paul's parents died, probably in a way unrelated to the persecution. He was exactly sixteen

years old and had a sister who was already married. According to these indications we can assume that the year of his
birth was approximately 234, which makes him considera-
bly older than Anthony, who was not born until after the
horrors of that persecution, around the year 251. Later Jerome even mentions a difference of twenty-three years
between their ages. Paul's parents are characterized as wealthy,
but, unlike Anthony, Paul is described as being extremely
well versed in Greek and Egyptian literature. In order to
escape the persecution, Paul withdrew to a country house.
But his brother-in-law had had designs on the property and
planned to denounce him. When Paul learned of this plan,
he decided to flee to the mountain wilderness and to await
there the end of the persecution. After changing his location several times, the young man stumbled onto a cave
that offered a spacious hall within. Not only that: there was
a spring and a palm tree within the hall, which was open
to the sky above. This cave was to become the hermit's
dwelling. The palm tree supplied him with food and clothing. Jerome immediately substantiates this by noting that
on his journeys he had met monks who had lived for many
decades on barley bread and water alone.

After these few facts about Paul's youth and his life as a
hermit, Jerome skips immediately to the end of the saint's
life and tells about the encounter between Anthony and
Paul that was captured also by many artists. He reports
that Saint Paul was already 113 years old, whereas Anthony
numbered "only" ninety years. As the story goes, it was
revealed to the latter in a dream that a hermit was staying
in the desert who was even more virtuous than he himself. Thereupon Anthony set out to find that holy man. A
centaur, a satyr, and a she-wolf supposedly showed him
the way to Paul's cave. Even Jerome expected that his contemporaries would be incredulous about the appearance of

these fabulous beasts and incidentally relates that a satyr, which he describes as a man with a crooked nose, horns, and cloven hooves, was once brought alive to Alexandria. Its body was allegedly preserved with salt and brought to Emperor Constantius in Antioch.

When he finally arrived at the cave of the proto-hermit, the latter at first did not want to open the door to let Anthony in. After much pleading, he did open the entrance to his cave and welcomed his confrere with an embrace and a kiss. Paul, who for decades had had no contact with civilization, wanted Anthony to tell him about everything.

During their conversation a raven flew in, bringing a loaf of bread. Paul told Anthony that every day for sixty years he had received half a loaf, and that the Lord was now doubling his ration. But instead of eating together, the two old monks argued until evening about whose prerogative it was to break the bread. After they agreed and were fortified by their meal, Paul revealed to his visitor why God had sent him to him: he, Anthony, was to bury the old hermit. But so that he might be able to die alone, Paul sent Anthony back to his monastery, where he was to fetch the cloak that Saint Athanasius had once given him. Paul wanted to wear it as his burial garment. Anthony hurried back, insofar as one can still speak of hurrying at his age. But while he was still on the second journey to Paul's cave, he suddenly saw in a vision how the hermit's soul, encircled by angels and surrounded by the choirs of the prophets and apostles, went up to heaven as white as snow.

The dead body, which Anthony found shortly afterward in the cave, remained in the posture of prayer: knees bent, body erect, and hands lifted up to heaven. On account of his age, however, Anthony did not think that he was capable of digging a grave for his friend. Then two lions came and relieved him of that task, only to flee again afterward with the blessing of the wizened Anthony. Anthony laid the dead body in the grave, covered it with earth, and set up a monument. Jerome also reports that Anthony took with him the tunic that Paul had made out of palm leaves and for the rest of his life wore it each year at Easter and Pentecost. Consequently these traditions must have originated from the circle of Anthony's disciples, and in fact at the beginning of his *Life* [*of Saint Paul, the First Hermit*] Jerome cites as his authority the disciples Amatas and Makarius, who had told him about Paul of Thebes.

The tradition goes on to report that the bones of the saintly proto-hermit, who is revered as the father of the eremitical life, were brought in 1381 to Buda in Hungary. Moreover, on Mount Sinai a monastery was founded that regards Paul as its model, and to this day there is an Order of Saint Paul the First Hermit.

FROM ANCHORITE TO CENOBITE—
PACHOMIUS

Whereas the solitude of the monk's cell that defined the type of the anchorite or hermit was still part of the monastic life of Anthony, a development began even during the lifetime of the Abbot toward a common life for monks and the founding of true monasteries. Now Anthony's brothers also lived in the loose association of a monastic settlement, yet strictly speaking they were hermits with individual cells. The new cloistered life was distinguished now by the fact that the monks lived together in one dwelling and the tasks assigned to them were also performed together. The leadership of the community was assumed by an abbot. The advantages of this way of life are plain to see: the brothers can support one another in their common prayer and labors and bear with one another in their spiritual life. The structured life of obedience and responsibility in a cloister allows for correction and, on occasion, the restraint of vice as well as the moderation of ascetic practices. It goes without saying that the common life also has its problems, which are spared the hermit. Quarrels, rivalries, self-will, and power struggles do not stop at the monastery walls. Laxity, too, or the wrong motivation for entering the monastery can seriously trouble a community. The great founders of religious orders responded to these basic problems of human coexistence by creating special rules.

Furthermore cloistered life does not permit that retreat into solitude which defines the eremitical state. This is

probably one reason why, even with the appearance and development of cloistered life, the eremitical state never completely disappeared, but to this day, through great saints like
Nicholas of Flüe or Charles de Foucauld, has maintained a
legitimate place in the variety of Christian ways of life.

Just as the eremitical existence is inseparably connected
with the name of Anthony, so too the beginnings of cloistered
life are bound up with that of Pachomius.

The facts about the life of Pachomius have been handed
down with much greater certainty than the information about
Paul of Thebes. Pachomius was born around the year 292
as the son of pagan parents in Upper Egypt. This is in the
first place a radical difference between him and Anthony.
The only thing that the two have in common is their Egyptian heritage. Whereas Anthony stood aloof from worldly
things even in his youth, Pachomius received an excellent
education and became a soldier. Now it is not certain
whether he belonged to Maximian's army or to Constantine's, nor does it matter that much for our purposes. The
important thing, rather, is that during an arduous military
campaign he ran into Christians; until that time he probably had had only secondhand knowledge about them, and
perhaps, if he was actually under Maximian's command, he
had even persecuted them. In any case these Christians, in
their unselfishness and neighborliness, made such a great
impression on young Pachomius that he inquired more
closely about their religion. Pachomius was fortunate that
the missionary zeal which is often so suspect to Christians
today was still taken for granted by the people whom he
asked. These simple Egyptian Christians brought about a
complete transformation in the young soldier's life. After
the conclusion of the aforementioned campaign, Pachomius promptly withdrew to a Christian village in the Thebaid. Here he enrolled in the group of catechumens who

were preparing for baptism and were being instructed in the Christian faith. We do not know how long this time of preparation lasted. Yet in that insignificant little village in the Thebaid, Pachomius received the sacrament of baptism. According to the old custom, he was confirmed at the same time with the sacred chrism and was allowed to participate for the first time in the sacred mysteries and to receive the Body of Christ. Pachomius was aware that the joy of his new status as a child of God was accompanied by solemn duties. Even in his youth he is said to have felt an inclination to solitude, which caused him after his baptism to go into the desert, where he visited the Greek hermit Palaemon, who like Anthony had a reputation for sanctity. The tradition reports that Pachomius remained for ten to twelve years in the school of Palaemon, where he was introduced to corporeal and spiritual asceticism and personally practiced them to a high degree of perfection.

Around the year 325 Pachomius was inspired by God to found in or near Tabennesi the first monastery in which the monks lived together under one roof and lived according to a common Rule, which Pachomius composed at the time of his first foundation. Unfortunately only fragments of the original Coptic text still exist. The early Greek translation has been lost as well. An Ethiopic version, however, has been preserved. The Latin translation was produced by Jerome. The aforementioned translations in the most widely used languages of the known world demonstrate the importance of this early monastic Rule. In particular it emphasizes poverty, fasting, common prayer, collaboration at work, silence, moderation, and discretion in eating, and the institution of a general chapter.

So many men thronged to the newly established monastery that soon almost one hundred monks had assembled. Thereupon Pachomius decided to found additional monasteries, seven or eight in all, among which the one in Paba was especially prominent and became the saint's residence. Two women's communities were also founded by the saint on the other bank of the Nile; Pachomius' sister was the first to enter the new foundation. The importance of the original monastery in Tabennesi was such, however, that the monks of Pachomius were also called Tabennesiots. By the time of Pachomius' death on May 14, 348, the number of monks is said to have reached almost seven thousand.

All the monasteries that the saint had founded were under his Rule and formed a community that bore the Greek name of *koinobion* (from *koinos bios*: common life). After the death of Pachomius the abbot of the principal monastery assumed the leadership of the community. Among his duties was the visitation of the daughter monasteries and presiding at the biennial assembly of all the monastic superiors.

Monastery life was organized according to Pachomius' religious Rule. Legend reports that he derived it from the instructions of an angel. As in the great Rules written later, the daily routine of the monks was divided into times of manual labor, prayer, and other pious exercises. Whereas a hermit had to worry only about supporting himself, now it was a matter of providing for a community. At the same time this meant a certain security for the individual. The manual labor consisted as always in basketmaking, the weaving of mats and blankets, and many other sorts of work, for instance, gardening. Again, as in the case of hermits, the income served not only as a livelihood but also as an opportunity to give alms. The monks ceased to use their worldly names and were called by their numbers; we see in this the beginnings of the custom of taking a religious name, which symbolizes renunciation of the world. The dozens of members in a monastery were subdivided into various classes, each of which was led by a superior and had a particular task in running the monastery. Every evening the monks gave their day's work to the superior, and once a week he in turn gave the products that were collected to the "econome", or treasurer of the monastery. From there they went to the business manager of the principal monastery, who also had the title of Grand Econome. Now it was his job to bring the products to market and to obtain the necessary materials and supplies for the monasteries.

We also learn something about the common life of these early cloistered monks. For instance, two or three brothers shared a cell. The brothers assembled for prayer and at mealtimes. The meager food had to be taken in silence, and the monks already wore wide cowls so that they could not look at each other. They wore over their shoulders a white goatskin called a *mēlotē*. The Greek word *mēlotē* basically means a "sheepskin"; it was an article of clothing worn by a prophet (see Mt 3:4; Heb 11:37). Pachomius' monks set aside their *mēlotēs* (recalling Gen 3:21) when Holy Mass was being celebrated, since it was regarded also as the garment of sinful man. Holy Communion was received on the first and last days of the week, i.e., Sundays and Saturdays. When a confrere died, special prayers and the Holy Sacrifice were offered for him. This shows the antiquity of the custom of offering Masses for the faithful departed.

In order to minimize the danger of accepting good-fornothings or shady characters into the community, it was necessary early on to introduce a time of probation for candidates to the "monastic state". This laid the groundwork for the novitiate—an indispensable, tried, and true period of discernment before full acceptance into the monastic community. Only after the novitiate was the candidate accepted through a ceremony in which he was clothed with

the religious habit and promised to follow the Rule. Pachomius, moreover, would not allow his monks to be ordained
priests, so as to avoid pride and envy. Out of humility he
himself refused ordination when it was offered to him. At
any rate men who were already ordained priests could be
admitted to the monastery so as to celebrate the holy mysteries there.

Although Pachomius was chiefly concerned with founding his monasteries and governing them, Bishop Serapion
of Tentyra managed to persuade him to have a church for
poor shepherds established in a nearby village, in which
Pachomius himself held the office of lector. We should
explain here that since early Christian times the Church
had, in addition to the higher orders (deacon, priest, bishop),
four lower orders as well, which have been retained in the
Eastern Rites and in communities that celebrate according
to the old rituals; the latter go by the names of porter
(doorkeeper), lector, exorcist, and acolyte; these are sacra-
mentals which bestow special graces on the ordained men
that enable them to perform special duties.

Besides these organizational achievements of Pachomius,
we must not forget the spiritual plane. He, like Anthony,
performed miracles in Christ's name and possessed prophetic abilities. And his renown, too, was so widespread
that around the year A.D. 333 he was visited by Athanasius,
with whom he was united by his solicitude for the Church
and his rejection of Arianism. The year 348 was to be especially momentous for the saintly founder of cloistered life.
First of all, on account of false accusations he was summoned before a synod of bishops in Latapolis, where he
was able to prove his innocence and virtue. Furthermore
his monastery was struck by the plague, which carried off
around a hundred of his monks and finally him, too. After
forty days of intense suffering the saint died. His *Vita* was

composed by an unknown monk shortly after his death and was supplemented by additional Coptic and Arabic accounts of his life. His *Life*, too, was translated into many languages and made Pachomius known far beyond the boundaries of Egypt.

The community founded by Pachomius continued to exist well into the eleventh century. Even in the twelfth century, more precisely around the year 1135, Anselm von Havelberg reported that he had seen in a monastery in Constantinople five hundred monks who lived according to the Rule of Pachomius.

SYRIA'S MARVELOUS FLOWERING
OF ASCETICISM—SIMEON STYLITES

Syria, the country surrounded by the civilizations of Egypt, Mesopotamia, and Asia Minor, never played an especially significant role in politics. Culturally its major cities were important for the traditions of the Near East. We will mention only Aleppo, Palmyra, Baalbek, Seleucia, Ugarit, Antioch, and Damascus. In particular Antioch, which was strongly hellenized, assumed great importance in the early Church, due primarily to the fact that the holy Apostle Simon Peter was the first bishop of that Syrian city before he went to Rome. From then on Antioch was reckoned as one of the four principal churches of the East and eventually developed into a patriarchate. The city's authority was strengthened by the lively missionary activity that proceeded from it and by the important theologians who succeeded Peter in the episcopal see of Antioch, such as Ignatius, Theophilus, and Serapion. At the same time the Church of Antioch became synonymous for the entire Syrian Church, and the Council of Nicaea acknowledged the special status of Antioch within the Universal Church of that time.

In Syria, too, various monastic movements developed, which we wish to examine now. In east Syria one peculiar feature was that celibacy was understood at first to be a requirement for all Christians. Since that, of course, was not sustainable, smaller communities developed that besides the vow of virginity also refrained from partaking of wine and meat and distinguished themselves from "common" Christians by their special garb. At the same time these "Sons of the Covenant" performed liturgical and ecclesiastical ministries, and one part of the clergy was selected from their numbers.

West Syrian monasticism, in contrast, sometimes assumed bizarre forms. Theodoret of Cyrus describes in his history of monasticism different forms of Syrian asceticism:

> Some of them fight [the good fight] in community; there are several thousand such monasteries. Others choose the eremitical life and are intent only on conversing with God. Others praise God by dwelling in tents and huts, and still others in dens and caves. Many do not even consent to own a cave or a tent or a hut but rather expose their bodies to the open air and endure the inclemency of the weather. Now they freeze in the extreme cold, now they burn under the scorching rays of the sun. . . . Some individuals stand without interruption, while others divide their day between sitting and praying. Some have walled themselves up and avoid converse with men, while others renounce such seclusion and are available to all who wish to see them.

Special notoriety was acquired in Syria by the holy men who were called Stylites. A Stylite spent many years of his life on a pillar, on the platform of which there was just enough room for him to stretch out. Many times a railing protected him from falling off the pillar while sleeping. On the other hand, they allowed no protective roof to ward off the sun or the rain.

But what was the origin of this strange custom, which had its imitators well into the nineteenth century? At the beginning of the Stylite movement was Simeon, who is generally distinguished from his numerous namesakes by the surname "Stylites". He was born in the late fourth century, probably between 388 and 391, in Sis, located on the border between Syria and Cilicia. Baptized while still a child and raised in the Christian faith, he at first tended his parents' sheep, without receiving an education. At the age of around fourteen he had an experience like Anthony's while attending church one Sunday and felt called by the Scripture reading to strive for Christian perfection. Around 403 he entered the monastery of Eusebona near Telada. His unusual zeal in prayer and asceticism met with disapproval from his older confreres, and Simeon left the monastery again in 412 and became a hermit in Telnesin in the vicinity of Antioch. At first he lived in a stone dwelling and devoted himself to asceticism. Like the holy hermits already mentioned, Simeon acquired various charismatic gifts, and many Christians and curious souls visited the holy man. We do not know whether his decision in 423 to spend the rest of his life on a pillar was a heavenly inspiration or whether it served instead to spare him the annoyance of visitors. At first the pillar was around three meters [ten feet] tall. The Stylite's reputation for holiness swiftly spread, and the number of visitors constantly increased. Simeon preached twice daily from the top of his pillar. After seven years the pillar was raised, and at the end of his life it is said to have been thirty meters [one hundred feet] high. Despite his restricted living space, he carried on an apostolate of converting pagans, making peace, and giving advice. The sources speak of entire clans that renounced their superstitions beneath his pillar and that became Christian. Simeon was concerned about morality in the surrounding parishes and also about maintaining the purity of the Christian faith. For instance, he vehemently championed the decisions of the Council of Chalcedon, which in 451 defended the doctrine of the two natures, declaring that Christ united in himself the Divine Nature and a human nature inseparably and without confusion. The saint died on September 2 in the year 459 at about the age of seventy. He had spent more than half his life on top of his pillar. After his death he was initially laid out for four days for public veneration and then brought in solemn procession to Antioch and entombed in the principal church of that city.

Although the Church sometimes criticized these forms of asceticism, which she regarded as sensationalism and vanity, they catered to a certain partiality of the Syrian people to things that are eccentric and extraordinary. After all, the whole purpose of them was to reach out to people and to win them over to the Gospel. And if some success was achieved in this eccentric way, then even the pillar, which in and of itself already symbolizes union with heaven, made sense. Furthermore, it must be noted that even in Syrian monasticism the Stylites were not the rule, and the large majority of ascetics lived an ordinary eremitical life instead. On a positive note it should also be emphasized that the Syrian monks were more closely involved in ecclesiastical life than those in Egypt, for example. Consequently many bishops were drawn from their ranks. Besides the strongly missionary character of the monasteries we should mention here also their charitable works, which consisted, for example, in the founding of hospitals and hostels for pilgrims.

MONASTICISM IN ASIA MINOR—
BASIL OF CAESAREA

Asia Minor, which was important already in biblical times, corresponds roughly to the Asian part of modern Turkey, or Anatolia, and was thus bounded by the Black Sea, the Marmara Sea, the Aegean Sea, and the eastern Mediterranean. Asia Minor, which served as the bridge between the Orient and the Occident, is among the oldest civilized regions in the world. The Christian faith arrived there as early as apostolic times through the missionary journeys of Paul, and numerous cities in Asia Minor are mentioned in Sacred Scripture, for example, Ephesus, Laodicea, and Philadelphia. The foundations for their well-defined ecclesiastical hierarchy were laid by the apostles themselves. Just as most major developments in the early Church proceeded from Asia Minor, so too it was the cradle of almost all the heresies.

Monasticism in Asia Minor, too, had a heretical leader: Eustathius of Sebaste and his followers not only refused to participate in the eucharistic celebrations of married priests but also proclaimed that no one could attain salvation unless he gave up all his property. They distinguished themselves by their dirty clothing and fasted paradoxically on Sundays. Of all people, a disciple of this Eustathius was to help Eastern monasticism become fully integrated into the Church: Basil of Caesarea. He would be just as important for monasticism in the Eastern Church as Benedict of Nursia (to be discussed later) for the Western Church, which is why he received the honorific title "Patriarch of the Greek Monks". The Basilians, who trace their origins back to him, are the most renowned religious order in the Eastern Church.

Basil was born in the year 329 in Caesarea in Cappadocia, the oldest of four sons, of whom three became bishops. His brother Gregory became a bishop in Nyssa; his brother Peter, Bishop of Sebaste, and he himself the bishop of his hometown. The remaining brother, Naucratius, chose the eremitical life but died while still in his youth. There were five sisters also, the oldest of whom consecrated her life to God. During the cruel persecutions of the Christians, several of the saint's ancestors suffered martyrdom. Basil grew up under the special care of his grandmother Macrina, who was herself a pupil of the Apostle of Cappadocia, Gregory the Thaumaturge [Wonder Worker]. Basil's formal education led him via Constantinople to Athens, where he made friends with Gregory Nazianzen. Along with his brother Gregory of Nyssa, the three friends later went on to become the three Cappadocian Fathers and were among the most important theologians of the fourth century. Around the year 355 Basil returned home and began to teach rhetoric in Caesarea. His sister Macrina, however, had such an influence on the scholar that he decided to give up worldly sciences and to devote himself to the ascetical way of life. Basil did not receive baptism until the age of around twenty-seven; afterward he traveled to the monastic colonies in Syria, Palestine, and Egypt, so as to become acquainted with the life of the monks there. After his return the holy man gave all his property to the poor and settled in the vicinity of Neocaesarea. The Egyptian monks were his most important models. At the same time Basil gathered like-minded men around him and founded several monasteries, in which he combined the anchoritic life with the cenobitic life. He thereby became the most important founder of monasticism

in Pontus and Cappadocia and of the Greek monastic tradition that continues to this day. Of lasting significance is
the Rule of Saint Basil, which unlike the Rule of Pachomius does not define every aspect of life in the monastery
but rather serves as a spiritual handbook for monastic life
that is based principally on Sacred Scripture. The *Asketikon*,
as the Rule is also called, comprises the Longer Rules and
the Shorter Rules. In 313 chapters the duties and obligations of a monk and the purpose of monastic life are presented in the form of a dialogue between the master and his
disciples. In so doing, Basil builds in part on the ideas of his
ascetical teacher Eustathius, whose heretical positions he has
of course rejected. The Rule, which Basil elaborated together
with Gregory Nazianzen, is distinguished by its humane moderation, which avoids all unnecessary severity. A certain flexibility and adaptability allows it to be applied to various forms
of monastic life. Basil's turn toward the cenobitic life goes
beyond mere practical and pedagogical reasoning and has
theological significance. It corresponds to the social nature
of man, who needs fellowship. Moreover, Basil has been
described, and not without good reason, as the "theologian
of the Holy Spirit", and in his theology of charisms, i.e., the
gifts of the Spirit, he especially highlights the Christian's vocation *for* the community. Precisely in this way the monastery,
too, should place its charisms at the service of the Universal
Church.

In Basil's monastery he and Gregory Nazianzen also pur-
sued their studies, which were so important, producing early
on the *Philokalia*, a florilegium or selection of quotations
from the writings of Origen. Despite their monastic seclusion, Basil followed the theological controversies of his time
and took an active part in the intellectual battles against
Arianism. Toward the end of 359 he undertook on his own
initiative a journey to Constantinople to oppose the Arian

Aetius. Although it grieved him, after his return he had to break off relations with his bishop, Dianios, since the latter had subscribed to an Arian formula. This rupture lasted until 362, when Dianios fell seriously ill and summoned Basil to his side in order to express to him his sincere remorse. Eusebius of Caesarea became Dianios' successor, and in 364 he ordained Basil a priest. From then on the latter exercised his ministry within the metropolitan see of Cappadocia, without giving up his ascetical way of life. In addition he continued to write on a wide variety of subjects; his development of the doctrine of the Trinity proved to be of lasting importance. In 370 the monk and theologian Basil was called to be Bishop of Caesarea.

Two years later Basil had to oppose Emperor Valens and the prefect Modestus, who were trying to bring Arianism back into favor in Cappadocia as well. In these controversies we see what a blessing it was that the monk—who was so closely united to God and, like Anthony before the judge, did not fear for his own life—would rather have faced death than betray the Gospel of Christ and the teaching of the Church. Together with Gregory Nazianzen and his brother Gregory of Nyssa, Basil honed the terminology of the Church's doctrine of the Trinity by making a clear distinction between nature and person. The one Divine Nature exists in three Persons who can be distinguished. "The peculiarity of the Father is that he is unbegotten, that of the Son that he is begotten, and that of the Spirit that he proceeds [from the other two]." Both the Son and the Spirit are of the same nature as the Father. At the Second Ecumenical Council of Constantinople in 381 the doctrine of the Trinity as clarified by the three great Cappadocian Fathers was confirmed and Arianism was definitively rejected. Basil, though, did not live to see it, since he died on January 1, 379, before even reaching the age of fifty. Like Saint Thomas

Aquinas, he had spent himself completely in his fight for the truth and the purity of the faith. Basil became a major and influential figure in the fields of homiletics and liturgy also. Outside the gates of Caesarea, moreover, he had founded a Christian charitable institution, which comprised a hospital, a lepers' asylum, a poorhouse, and a hostel.

FROM THE ORIENT TO THE OCCIDENT—MONASTICISM IN THE WEST

Even though we planned to deal principally with the life and work of the Desert Fathers, we should take a look at the development of the monastic ideal in the Western Church. In doing so we must not forget that the example of the Desert Fathers was an important factor here as well. In particular because of the many pilgrims who visited the monks in Egypt and Palestine, and also the writings that recounted the lives of eminent figures like Anthony, Western Christians were fascinated by the ascetical life. Nevertheless Western monasticism was not merely a subsidiary of the Eastern variety but rather has its own history and its own distinct forms, which we will discuss shortly. One foundation pillar of Western monasticism was familial asceticism, in other words, the ascetical life of a Christian within his family. The transition to a truly monastic life was accomplished around the middle of the fourth century. Besides the itinerant ascetics, who at times were scurrilous and prone to discredit monasticism because of their lack of refinement, it was mainly members of the nobility, in Rome for example, who showed interest in the ascetical life. Initially we find groups of women in aristocratic circles whose teacher was the aforementioned theologian Saint Jerome, who stayed in Rome during the years 382–384. The center of that early conventual movement was

the house of the wealthy widow Marcella on the Aventine
Hill. From there a great number of men and women set out
for Palestine so as to live in cloistered community in the vicinity of the holy places. The first one mentioned [in his corre-
spondence] is Melania the Elder, who in 380 founded a double
monastery for women and men on the Mount of Olives. A
few years later, around 385, Jerome followed her, along with
Paula the Elder and her daughter Eustochium. Together
Paula and Jerome founded a double monastery in Bethlehem,
whereby Paula became the superior of the women's monastery and Jerome the superior of the men's monastery. Before
founding their monasteries, both Jerome and Paula visited the
monks in the Nitrian Desert so as to learn from them.

Meanwhile, back at Rome, with Jerome's departure the
community moved its place of residence to the countryside,
and from then on the country villa became the preferred
location for many new monasteries, far from the hustle and
bustle of the city. Yet at the same time the "urban monastery" continued and became established as a type. In the
fifth century this form of monastery was adopted by the
Roman popes and further developed into the basilica monastery, in which a monastic community placed itself at the
service of a particular house of worship. In the rest of Italy,
too, monastic life became increasingly important. Thus Bishop
Eusebius of Vercelli, for example, lived with his clerics in an
ascetical household and created the type of the clerical monastery. Ambrose of Milan, the influential bishop and Doctor
of the Church, made his episcopal see into a monastic center with several monasteries. Although Ambrose himself was
not a monk, his spiritual writings became a guide for Western monasticism. He also reports that there were settlements
of hermits on the islands along the Italian coast. Additional
foundations followed. The Italian monastery of Pinetum near
Terracina received from Rufinus of Aquileia the Rule of

Saint Basil, which was thus able to bear fruit in the Christian West as well. In Campania and Sicily, Melania the Younger founded several monasteries.

The peculiarities of Western monasticism were due to its promotion by the nobility, as previously mentioned; therefore, entering a monastery meant a rise in social status for former slaves, for instance. In the West, moreover, influential bishops were in the first place the ones who promoted the monastic idea and provided material support. This resulted in a closer connection between the monastery and the Church hierarchy than we have seen in the East. Monasticism also acquired thereby a certain flexibility, which led to a closer adaptation to the given ecclesiastical situation. Another considerable difference is the minimal importance of the eremitical life in the West.

Whereas in Italy it was the Bishop Ambrose of Milan who was especially preeminent in promoting monasticism, in North Africa it was his most influential student, Saint Augustine of Hippo. In his younger years the later saint and Doctor of the Church went far astray in the religious and moral sense, to the sorrow of his mother, Saint Monica. Besides the prayers of his saintly mother and the persuasive power of Saint Ambrose, the reputation of our Saint Anthony played an important role in his conversion, which enabled him to become one of the most famous defenders of the Catholic faith. And so the convert, after his return to North Africa, unhesitatingly transformed his parents' house in Thagaste into a monastery. Even when he was ordained a priest in 390 and consecrated a bishop in 396, Augustine persevered in the monastic way of life and urged his clergy as well to live in community. Western monasticism is indebted to the Bishop of Hippo not only for his monastic foundations and his spiritual writings, but also for one of the most important Rules of monastic life.

ROMAN-OCCUPIED GAUL—
MARTIN OF TOURS AND
JOHN CASSIAN

In the fourth century, Gaul, too, was to become especially important for Western monasticism. Not the least significant factor was Saint Anthony, whose renown reached as far as Trier. In addition there were influences from Spain, where a radical asceticism had developed under Bishop Priscillian. Once again these ideas made their way chiefly through aristocratic circles and traveled via Poitiers to Tours. In Tours, above all, the well-known Saint Martin would become the leading figure of Gallic monasticism. Born around 316 or 317 in Sabaria as the son of pagan parents, he resettled as a child in the Italian district of Pavia. At the early age of fifteen he became a Roman soldier. While still a catechumen he experienced that fateful encounter with a freezing beggar, to whom he gave half of his cloak. Afterward Christ appeared to him in a dream, wearing the beggar's half cloak. At the age of eighteen Martin was baptized, and a few years later he withdrew to Poitiers and was ordained an exorcist by Saint Hilary. After subsequent stays in Pannonia, where he converted his mother to the Christian faith and opposed Arianism, and Milan, Martin retreated together with a priest to the little island of Gallinaria near Genoa as a hermit. In 360, when Bishop Hilary returned again to Poitiers after several years in exile, he granted Martin a piece of land. On it the holy man established the first monastery in Gaul: the monastery in Ligugé. Sulpicius Severus, Martin's contemporary and biographer, reports that Martin raised a man from the dead and worked many other miracles in his monastery. After the death of Bishop Lidorius of Tours around 371 or 372, the citizens of Tours compelled the unwilling monk to assume the office of bishop. All of Martin's attempts to escape failed. Even the geese in the barn where the monk was hiding would not allow the holy man to evade his vocation and betrayed him with their loud honking. To this day "Martin's geese" recall this "betrayal" on the saint's feast day.

As bishop, Martin built his second monastery in nearby Marmoutier, so as to be able to continue his monastic life. The monks' existence in wooden cells or caves still strongly resembled eremitical life, and yet the communal aspect was also clearly evident. Not even the community owned any property; general church funds paid for their support. Among the tasks of the younger brothers was transcribing books. There were as many as eighty brothers in the monastery in Marmoutier; quite a few of them subsequently were themselves called to minister as bishops, and through his extensive influence Martin became the Apostle of Gaul, which was still largely pagan. On November 11, 397 (or 400), Martin died, and his grave in Tours, over which a basilica was constructed in later years, became an important place of pilgrimage. The monk and bishop became an especially popular saint, and only Nicholas of Myra is as well known as Martin among Christian children, thanks to pious customs.

In southeastern Gaul, specifically in the Rhône valley, in Marseilles and on the Mediterranean islands along the coast, a particular form of monasticism developed that was independent of the movement started by Martin of Tours. For instance, Honoratus, who had become acquainted with Eastern monasticism during his travels as a student, founded an island monastery in Lérins between 405 and 410. Yet here, too, Eastern monasticism was not simply adapted; Rhône monasticism had its own peculiar features. Here too the men who gathered in community were mostly members of the old Gallo-Roman aristocracy who had been driven south by the Teutons. In these monasteries asceticism, scholarship, and culture combined, and the episcopal sees in southern Gaul were occupied predominantly by monks, who in turn promoted monasticism in their dioceses and founded new monasteries. We should emphasize here, for example, the later Bishop Caesarius of Arles, who wrote the first Rule specifically for a monastery of nuns.

An eminent figure in the early fifth century was the monk and priest John Cassian, whom we learn about both from his own writings and also from the literary historian Gennadius of Marseilles. Born around 360 in the Romanian region of Dobruja, this scholar grew up in a Christian environment and received a thorough education. At the age of twenty, Cassian set out with his friend Germanus on a pilgrimage to Palestine. Fascinated by Palestinian monasticism, they entered a monastery near Bethlehem, where they completed their novitiate and professed religious vows. There, in the immediate vicinity of the Grotto of the Nativity, where the Eternal Word appeared visibly in the flesh, the friends spent four years. Yet over the course of the years they became disillusioned; they found no one in their monastery who taught and practiced the ascetical ideal as they would have liked. The mediocrity of the monastery prompted the friends in 385 to visit the Desert Father in Egypt so as to become better acquainted with the path of purification and perfection. With a heavy heart their abbot let them go, but only after they promised to return again. John and

Germanus visited the monks in the Nile Delta as well as those in Kellia and Sketis. After seven years, in 392, the friends went back, as they had promised, for a short time to their monastery in Bethlehem and obtained a release from their promise to return forever to that community. Cassian and Germanus traveled once again to Sketis and the Theban desert, where they met the monks of Saint Anthony. Cassian later wrote down what he learned about the life and teaching of the monks. He thereby brought the essential doctrines of the Desert Fathers into the Latin-speaking world. He himself saw in them the embodiment of Christian perfection. Since he had a good command of both Greek and Latin, he very capably assumed this role of mediator between East and West. Besides accounts of the life and ascetical teachings of the monks, we owe to Cassian especially the tradition of the hesychasm (from the Greek word *hesycha*: quiet, stillness). This prayer of quiet, consisting of the constant, meditative repetition of a verse, is the first step in formation for the Prayer of the Heart, or the Jesus Prayer. As the name already clearly indicates, its purpose is to attain profound exterior and interior quiet and to overcome the limitations that keep the soul from God. The one who prays it experiences an encounter with his Creator and Redeemer and from this source of strength can shape his life. Whereas the traditional prayer of quiet is practiced to this day in the East, especially on Mount Athos, this treasure remains to be brought back again to the West.

Cassian's most important spiritual teacher was Evagrius Ponticus, a disciple of Origen. After the death of his teacher (399) and the expulsion of the Origenist monks, Cassian and Germanus left Egypt in 401 and traveled to Constantinople, where they became disciples of the great patriarch John Chrysostom. He also ordained Cassian a deacon. The latter was admitted to priestly ordination around 405 in Rome, when he spoke to Pope Innocent I in defense of Chrysostom, who meanwhile had been banished. After 410 Cassian arrived in Marseilles (Germanus is no longer mentioned) and with the support of the bishop Proclus founded in 415 the monastery of Saint Victor [the later Abbey of Saint Victor] and the Convent of the Holy Savior. Cassian governed the monastery as abbot until his death. At the behest of Pope Leo the Great, with whom he had probably been on friendly terms since his stay in Rome, the scholar composed in 430 a treatise against the heresy of Nestorius. Cassian died around the year 435 and was entombed in the crypt in Saint Victor. The Diocese of Marseilles and the Greek Church revere him as a saint. His great endeavor was to make Eastern monastic life, in a somewhat mitigated and modified form, at home in the West. Especially effective in this regard were his writings *The Institutes of Cenobitic Life*, in which he describes Eastern monastic life, and his *Conferences with the Fathers* (*Collationes Patrum*), which he composed between 425 and 429. These writings were so important that Benedict later incorporated them into his Rule and had the *Collationes* read aloud to his monks after mealtimes. An excerpt from the monastic precepts of John Cassian was also used in the monasteries of Southern Gaul.

IRISH MONASTICISM—
PATRICK AND COLUMBAN

Besides the monasticism of Martin and of the Rhône Valley, a third type of monk in the region of Gaul should be
mentioned, which for the sake of simplicity we will call
Irish. It is quite probable, however, that this type was originally influenced by Gallic monasticism. At the beginning
of the movement stood the Briton Patrick (ca. 385–461),
who was to become the Apostle of Ireland. Patrick was
born in Bannavem Taberniae in Roman Brittany. Around
401 he was kidnapped by plundering Irishmen and taken
back to their island, where for several years he was enslaved
and tended sheep. Meanwhile he became acquainted with
the indigenous people of that isle and learned their language. Moreover Patrick experienced those years as a time
of reflection and conversion. After six years Patrick was able
to escape and return safely to his British home. The traditions about the following years are somewhat vague. It is
supposed that Patrick went first as a monk to Southern Gaul
and lived there in the famous monastery in Lérins. Later he
is said to have become a cleric in Auxerre. In a dream he
heard a call to go back to Ireland. This calling was fulfilled
in 432, when he was appointed successor to the first Irish
missionary bishop, Palladius. After being consecrated a bishop,
the holy man made the crossing with twenty-four companions and settled on the Hibernian isle. Tradition still has it
that when Patrick set foot on Irish soil, all the snakes and

poisonous animals left the island, and this theme became, along with his bishop's attire, an important emblem in portraying the Apostle of Ireland. Despite the opposition of the pagan Druids, Patrick converted thousands of people, as he himself relates in his *Confession*. To illustrate the mystery of the Trinity he is said to have used a three-leafed clover, which became the national symbol of Ireland. In general, Patrick was a missionary who won over souls to the Christian faith with the help of powerful symbols. At Easter in 433 he kindled a fire on a hill that was visible far and wide, so as to mark the victory of the light of Christ over the darkness. In 449 the monk Patrick made a forty-day retreat in solitude on a mountain in County Mayo. On that mountain, which today bears the name of Croagh Patrick and is one of the most popular places of pilgrimage in Ireland, Patrick wrested from an angel a promise that he himself would be allowed to judge his beloved Irishmen at the Last Judgment.

When Saint Patrick died in 461, Ireland not only had been Christianized but also had an ecclesiastical organization, whereby the metropolitan see of Armagh, located in the north, also became the ecclesiastical center of Ireland. The unique feature of Ireland was the monastic character of church life in its entirety. There were the great saintly monastic founders like Finnian, Columban the Elder of Hy, Comgall of Bangor, Brendan, Kevin, and Columban the Younger; the Christian faith took root in Ireland largely because they played an essential part in planting it. Scattered all over the island monasteries were built in which men lived a life of strict asceticism combined with learned scholarship. Ireland became the Island of Saints and the Island of Scholars. The island was inhabited and ruled by numerous tribes or clans, and each clan had a monastery as the center of its ecclesiastical life. The abbots of the major monasteries became at the same time the real leaders of the Irish Church. Since they themselves lacked episcopal consecration, they frequently had one of their monks consecrated as a bishop to ordain priests for the community. All aspects of pastoral work were carried out by the monks, who accordingly had to be priests. In contrast to the Egyptian monks, in Ireland the monk-priest was the norm.

These facts led to a development that would prove to be a blessing for the entire Western Church. In earlier centuries a serious sinner had to confess a public sin (i.e., one that was generally known) publicly in the presence of the congregation, or a secret sin to the bishop. The bishop then imposed on him a penance that could last a rather long time, sometimes several years. Only after the time of penance was the sinner absolved and accepted again into full communion with the Church, so that he could receive the sacraments. This reconciliation was possible only once in a lifetime. Yet in the monasteries, even in the early days, the practice of frequent private confession and voluntary penance had developed, which facilitated striving for perfection. Now this way of living the faith was requested also by the faithful who lived outside the monastery, and thus the practice of private confession developed, which is commonly used to this day. This includes the personal admission of all sins, while the absolution follows directly afterward. In order to regulate this new practice, guidebooks for confessors developed first in Ireland; these consisted of a catalogue of sins and the corresponding penances to be imposed. These guidebooks later spread throughout the Western Church. Through the fruitful pastoral work of the monk-priests and the renewed custom of frequent confession, Ireland itself attained a high level of religious practice and morality, which exerted an influence on the mainland as well.

Irish monasticism always retained an anchoritic character. Many monks sought the solitude of the islands off the Irish coast. The Skelligs, two small rock islands [Little Skellig and Skellig Michael, or Great Skellig] without vegetation, presented the greatest challenge. Even today Skellig Michael, for example, can be reached only by boat when the sea is calm. Skillfully designed stone stairways lead to the former monks' cells, which are exposed to the primordial forces of nature. The first monks had to bring fertile soil with them to the islands so as to be able to start at least a small garden.

Whereas banishment from the tribe and from the island was considered the worst punishment imaginable for an Irish clan member, the voluntary renunciation of home and family became the ideal of the monk. Just as Abraham once left Ur in Chaldea, so too the Irish monks were drawn to *peregrinatio*, to pilgrimage. This act of leaving one's home could consist in settling on one of the islands just mentioned. But more often the missionary zeal of the monks drew them to the mainland. They attracted the attention of the indigenous population by their very appearance: their heads were shaven on top and encircled with a crown of hair, while the hair at the back of their heads fell in long, flowing tresses. Besides a long pilgrim's staff they carried with them a flask of water and a leather bag which held, most importantly, the necessary books. Around his neck a monk-priest carried a reliquary and a small container in which to store consecrated Hosts. They never stayed long in one place but rather always felt compelled to keep traveling and to tell other people about Christ. Hence their mission did not have the same breadth and deep-seated effectiveness as the later, more systematic mission of the Anglo-Saxons, whose most important representative would be Saint Boniface. Nevertheless the monasteries founded by the Irish monks served as centers of Christian education in the midst of a populace that was still almost entirely heathen.

The most important monastic founder of the Scotch-Irish missionary movement on the mainland was Columban the Younger (530–615). Born in the east Irish province of Leinster, Columban entered the monastery in Bangor (located on the southern shore of Belfast Lough in the province of Ulster) under Abbot Comgall, its founder. At the age of around sixty, Columban, following Christ's example, went on a holy pilgrimage with twelve companions and crossed over to the mainland. He traveled through Brittany, Gaul, and Burgundy, promoting the missions and working for religious and moral renewal, especially among the nobility and the clergy. He founded his first monasteries in the Vosges: Anegrey, Luxeuil, and Fontaine. For these monasteries he composed a strict rule that was based entirely on his own strict ascetical way of life. Yet, precisely by this strictness he attracted many young men, who were inspired by the monastic ideal and entered his monasteries. Each motherhouse in turn also influenced the immediate and more remote vicinity and recorded additional new foundations governed by Columban's rule. Starting from Fontaine alone fifty new monasteries were founded on the mainland. When Columban, like John the Baptist and many other saints, opposed the immorality at the royal court of the Merovingian king Theuderich II around the year 610, he had to leave the motherhouse in Luxeuil and flee to Alemannia, which was still largely pagan. The monk settled for a short time in Bregence then crossed the Alps in 613 to continue his work in Northern Italy. Columban the Younger died in the year 615 in the Abbey of Bobbio, which he had founded.

Columban's work was to become very influential. He not only had showed insular monasticism the way to the mainland but also had established ties between his monasteries and the nobility. Of all the social strata, the landed aristocracy in the late sixth century proved to be remarkably receptive to the monastic-ascetical ideal, in which they found a new purpose in life. Columban's strict rules neither define the monastery's organization nor give an exact description of the everyday monastic regimen; therefore, later Western monasticism relied mainly on mixed/hybrid rules which supplemented Columban's rules. The close connection between the bishops and the monasteries in the West also led to an enrichment of ecclesiastical life, which did not exist in that form in the East. After the official Christianization of the Roman Empire, many of the new Christians did not experience a real *conversio*, which is why this concept came to be connected with entering a monastery. Whereas in the pre-Constantinian era all Christians were members of the Militia Christi, Christ's army, now this term was exclusively associated with monasticism. At the same time a call to true conversion went out from the monasteries into the world. The monasteries played an essential role in the actual Christianization of the world that now called itself Christian.

BENEDICT OF NURSIA—FATHER OF WESTERN MONASTICISM

When the Holy Father, Benedict XVI, chose his papal name, two interpretations were assigned to this choice: the Pope, commentators said, wanted to recall and associate himself with his great predecessors in the papacy, especially with Benedict XV, the Pope of Peace. Furthermore he wanted to recall that monk who stood at the beginning of the Christian West: Benedict of Nursia. Although, as in the case of Anthony, there were monks and monasteries even before him, Benedict—whom Pope Paul VI proclaimed a patron saint of Europe in 1964—was to become the real father of Western monasticism; indeed, even the honorific titles "Father of the West" or "Father of Europe" have been assigned to this simple monk from Central Italy.

Benedict was born around 480 with his twin sister, Scholastica, in Nursia, modern Norcia, in Italy, as the son of an aristocratic family. The most important source for Benedict's *Life* is a biographical description by Pope Gregory the Great, which he records in the second of his four books of *Books of Dialogues*. The stages of Benedict's life presented by Gregory also depict the saint's interior journey. While still a youth Benedict was sent by his parents to Rome for his education. Living in that city, which was already markedly decadent in every respect, horrified Benedict so much that he decided to leave Rome and bid farewell to the world. At first he was welcomed by a group of ascetics in Affile (modern Enfide) in the Sabine Mountains near Rome. Yet Benedict, too, was drawn at first to complete solitude. This he found in a narrow cave near Subiaco, situated east of Rome and north of Anagni on the Teverone. For three years the young ascetic stayed in that cave, which was later called the Holy Grotto. The monk Romanus, who lived in the neighboring monastery of Vicovaro, brought bread each day and lowered it to him on a rope. Benedict himself wanted to devote himself entirely to asceticism, following the example of the Egyptian Desert Fathers. And he experienced the challenges and temptations that Anthony encountered. The temptations of the flesh are said to have been so strong that the monk rolled naked in thorns in order to be rid of them. As a result he obtained from God a perfect tranquility that showed the success of his ascetical efforts. When the hermit was found in his cave by shepherds, they mistook him at first for a wild beast. It quickly became clear to them, however, that they were not dealing with an irrational creature but rather with a saint who lived in that hole in the ground. From then on they brought him food, and Benedict taught the shepherds about the path to sanctity. His reputation spread swiftly in the surrounding area, and the monks of Vicovaro even elected him their abbot. Like Anthony and Martin, Benedict was reluctant at first to accept the office. When he finally assumed that responsibility he soon noticed that laxity—at least according to his standards—prevailed in this monastery, and he tried to counteract it by discipline and order. Indeed, saints are people with whom everyone would like to be acquainted but who do not always make pleasant neighbors and contemporaries, since they expect from those who turn to them for assistance the same strictness that they impose on themselves. As we have already hinted, saints are not the only ones who live behind the

walls of a cloister, and some inmates of the monastery felt
that their comfortable existence was disrupted to such an
extent by the new abbot that they did not shrink from
poisoning his wine. When Benedict made the sign of the
cross over his cup before drinking it, as was his custom, it
shattered. Alerted by this incident, the monk left the monastery and retreated again for a while to his cave. Now,
however, he was joined by many brothers who wanted to
attain Christian perfection under his guidance. Benedict
founded twelve monasteries, with twelve monks living in
each, and placed them under the Rule of Pachomius. They
exist to this day. Yet in this endeavor also he encountered
the envy and jealousy of a priest from the vicinity, who
tried not only to slander and poison the saint but also to
lead his disciples astray. Benedict evaded this unproductive
conflict and left Subiaco.

This apparent flight in the year 529 was to become a
blessing for Western monasticism and the Church, since
Benedict had decided to move to Monte Cassino. On that
mountain there was still a pagan temple in which Apollo
and Venus were revered. The holy man completely erad-
icated the pagan idolatry. Superstitious fear yielded to fear
of God, and Benedict founded his most important monastery, which to this day is the center of the Benedictine
Order. The founding of this monastery and the closing of
the Platonic Academy by Emperor Justinian that same year
are regarded by many historians as the end of pagan antiquity and the beginning of the Christian Middle Ages.
Henceforth Benedict worked in his monastery and from
there founded additional monasteries as well. Besides
his virtuousness and holiness, his power to work miracles,
his gift of prophecy, and his ability to read hearts became
renowned far beyond the confines of Monte Cassino.
Probably around 540 Benedict composed the Rule that is

inseparably connected with his name and that, alongside
Augustine's instructions, acquired lasting significance in Western monasticism. In response to the many symptoms of
disintegration in the slowly decaying society of late antiquity, he held up the ideal of constancy. Moreover his monasteries promoted interethnic unity, since Romans and
Teutons, for example, lived under the same roof. Tradition
even relates that between 542 and 546 the king of the Goths,
Totila, visited the holy man, who foretold the monarch's
death.

Benedict himself was stricken on March 15, 543, with a
serious fever. Six days later he ordered his brothers to carry
him to the monastery church so that he could receive the
sacraments of the dying. After he had received the Viaticum,
he died while standing and praying. His body was buried
at first in his monastery, but after the destruction of the
monastery by the Langobards tradition has it that the holy
man's remains and those of his sister, Scholastica, were transferred to the monastery of Fleury [originally Fleury Abbey]
in France. That monastery then took the name of Saint-
Benoît-sur-Loire. Major relics of the saint are revered today
in Solesmes, Einsiedeln, Montpellier, Benediktbeuern, and
Metten.

Benedict's fruitful work on behalf of monasticism, the
Church, and all of Western culture must not be underesti-
mated. The many honorific titles that we have already mentioned testify to this fact. In 590 for the first time a
Benedictine, Gregory the Great, became Pope. Both the
Benedictine Orders, from which the Cistercians developed
as a reformed order, and also the Rule of Saint Benedict
spread throughout the Catholic world. Benedict's monastery was devastated on several other occasions. In 1349 it
was destroyed by an earthquake and subsequently rebuilt.
In 1944 the Allies completely destroyed the monastery by

their bombing attacks, since they suspected that the Germans had placed artillery in the monastery. Fortunately a German officer was able to bring an architect's drawings of the abbey and valuable art treasures to Rome before the bombardment, and it was possible to reconstruct the monastery completely.

CONCLUSION—RELIGIOUS ORDERS AND THE RENEWAL OF THE CHURCH

Already in the early centuries that we have examined, monasticism and the movement to found religious orders repeatedly gave new incentive and vitality to the whole Church. The Christianization of entire peoples would be almost inexplicable without the persistent work of the monasteries. Not only physics teaches that a mass is prone to inertia. Thus again and again among Christians as well one finds the effort to settle down in this world and to have it good. In contrast the monk and the ascetic are like the uncomfortable thorn in the flesh; they plainly deny the self-sufficiency of earthly life and of this world and deliberately prefer a renunciation that can be explained only by the hope of heaven and eternal life. The monk's self-denial begins radically in precisely those departments of life which have perennially seemed to be the most important: ownership, self-determination, and sexuality. At the same time those who admonish so uncomfortably become the salt that lends Christianity its original savor.

The history of monasticism and religious life is also a history of constant reconsideration and new beginnings. Even Anthony made it clear that one does not simply become an ascetic and then remain so forever; instead, the ascetic is challenged to begin his asceticism anew each day so as not to slacken. The same is true on a large scale. The entire history of religious orders is marked by subsequent reflections and new beginnings. Let us look, for example, at the Benedictine Order, which over the centuries increased in size and significance. This was accompanied by the accumulation of property and also by a certain worldliness, problems that Saints Robert of Molesme, Stephen Harding, and Bernard of Clairvaux responded to in the late eleventh and early twelfth centuries by founding and organizing the Cistercian Order, a reformed Benedictine Order that started in the Abbey of Cîteaux and demanded stricter observance of the Rule of Benedict. In the seventeenth century the Cistercian Order gave rise in turn to the Trappist Order, which again strove to return to the strict monastic life of Cîteaux and consequently regarded itself as the Cistercians of the strict observance. Much of their life was reminiscent of the strict asceticism of the Egyptian hermits described at the beginning of our reflections. Besides solemn prayer in choir, the Trappists practiced strict silence, which was facilitated by the development of their own sign language. Their asceticism consisted in abstaining from meat, fat, eggs, and wine, and in various ascetical practices. The monks lived by manual labor and did not have individual cells. Scholarship was regarded with a certain disdain. The Camaldolese Hermits, founded at the beginning of the eleventh century, are another reformed branch of the Benedictines.

Just as the saints are God's specific answer to the needs of a given time, so too are the religious orders that have been founded over the course of the centuries. We can mention only a few important movements. In the eleventh century Bruno of Cologne (ca. 1030–1101) founded the one Catholic religious order that has never required reform and has always faithfully maintained its initial strictness and ideals: the Carthusian Order. This order combines the life of the hermit (individual cells) and that of the cenobite (prayer in choir, common meals on Sundays and feast days, and a weekly stroll). Around 1185 a band of hermits headed by Bertold of Calabria on Mount Carmel developed into the Carmelite Order. At first this community had an eremitical character, but later it conformed to the way of life of the mendicant orders.

Certainly the most important medieval orders are the mendicant orders, which were founded by Saint Francis of Assisi and Saint Dominic. Inspired in part by the Crusaders, who spread the idea of following Christ in poverty and penitence, and also in reaction to a worldly Christianity that had grown all too lukewarm, an unprecedented movement of evangelical poverty began in the Church at the turn of the thirteenth century. Broad sectors of the population devoted themselves to reading the Bible. The wealth and worldliness of clerics and religious were censured, and the ideal of evangelical poverty was upheld. While several movements starting within the Church during that era overshot the mark and went to heretical extremes (for instance, the Waldenses), the principal danger to the Church was posed by the unchristian sects like the Cathari or the Albigensians. This is where Francis and Dominic came in. After a turbulent youth, Francis (1181 or 1182–1226) experienced a profound conversion that prompted him, after several years as a hermit, to found a community that would live in total evangelical poverty and bring the Gospel to the world. The Friars Minor, or Little Brothers, were born, and Francis traveled with his companions not only across Italy, where he attended to the Cathari, in particular, but even to Egypt to see the Sultan and to preach to him about the love of Christ. In 1224 Francis received the stigmata of Christ, and he died on October 3, 1226. From his original foundation developed the Poor Clare Nuns and the Capuchin Friars, among other religious orders.

Dominic (1170–1221), in contrast to Francis, was a priest. When he observed on journeys with his bishop the devastating effect of the Cathari on the Christian people, he decided to found a religious order that would likewise live in evangelical poverty and work for the conversion of the heretics. In 1216 the Order of Preachers, as the Dominicans are officially called, was approved by Pope Innocent III. Their strict poverty was combined with an obligation to complete a thorough theological education. Over the years the Dominican Order, which also started a female branch, likewise developed into a mendicant order after the example of the Franciscans.

In 1534 Ignatius of Loyola (1491–1556) together with six companions founded the Society of Jesus, which came to be known as the Jesuit Order. To the three vows of poverty, obedience, and chastity they added a special vow of obedience to the Pope. A Jesuit was supposed to be able to serve the Church freely, and so there was no requirement for community prayer or a special religious habit. A particularly intensive course of study enabled the Jesuits to distinguish themselves not only in preaching and spiritual direction but especially in teaching and in defending the faith, above all, during the Counter-Reformation.

We could mention here many other religious communities that came into being precisely when the needs of the time demanded it. The nineteenth century alone brought forth hundreds of charitable and apostolic movements. Some of these foundations are already well past their prime or no longer exist. Other communities, in contrast, are of lasting importance for the Church, which can be seen from reports of their increasing numbers and large novitiate classes. Interestingly enough, this is less true of those orders that had nothing more urgent to do than to conform themselves to the secular world, but it certainly applies to the old contemplative orders, which represent a timelessness and reliability that are not subject to quickly changing fashions and trends. In an age of hectic activity, apathy, and changes, someone who is seeking God will not flee from a secularized world into a secularized cloister, but rather expects from a religious community that constancy that Saint Benedict, in his similarly superficial age, left to his order as a legacy. It is that constancy which the first hermits sought in the solitude of their caves and grottos and without which the monk cannot find himself, much less the way to God.

SELECTED BIBLIOGRAPHY

Athanasius. *The Life of Antony: The Coptic Life and the Greek Life.* Translated by Tim Vivian and Apostolos N. Athanassakis. Kalamazoo, Mich.: Cistercian Publications, 2003.

Dyckhoff, Peter. *Einübung in das Ruhegebet: Eine christliche Praxis nach Johannes Cassian.* 2 vols. Munich: Don Bosco Verlag, 2006.

Frank, Karl Suso. *Askese und Mönchtum in der alten Kirche.* Darmstadt: Wissenshaftliche, 1975.

Frank, Karl Suso. *Grundzüge der Geschichte des christlichen Mönchtums.* Darmstadt: Wissenshaftliche, 1975.

Franzen, August. *Kleine Kirchengeschichte.* Freiburg: Herder, 2000.

Friess, Peer, ed. *Auf den Spuren des heiligen Antonius.* Memmingen: Verlag Memminger Zeitung, 1994.

Jerome. *Trois vies de moines: Paul, Malchus, Hilarion.* Paris: Cerf, 2007.

Lanczkowski, Johanna. *Kleines Lexikon des Mönchtums.* Stuttgart: Reclam Verlag, 1993.

Nigg, Walter. *Vom Geheimnis der Mönche.* Zurich: Artemis, 1953.

Puzicha, Michaela. *Benedikt von Nursia begegnen.* Augsburg: Sankt Ulrich Verlag, 2004.

Queffélec, Henri. *St. Anthony of the Desert.* Translated from the French by James Whitall. New York: Dutton, 1954.

Sartory, Gertrude and Thomas, eds. *Antonios der Grosse: Stern der Wüste.* Freiburg: Herder, 1989.

Schatz, Klaus. *Geschichte des Ordenslebens.* Lecture WS 85/86. University of Bamberg.

Steidle, Basilius, ed. *Antonius Magnus Eremita 356–1956. Studia Anselmiana.* Fasc. 38. Rome: S. Anselmi, 1956.

Trebbin, Heinrich. *Sankt Antonius: Geschichte, Kult und Kunst.* Frankfurt: Haag and Herchen, 1994.

Von Hertling, Ludwig *Antonius der Einsiedler.* Innsbruck: Felizian Rauch, 1929.

INDEX

MEDITERRANEA

Alexandria

NITRIAN
DESERT

Pispir

Queman

Monast
Saint